SWIMMING
A HANDBOOK FOR TEACHERS

Swimming

a handbook for teachers

HELEN ELKINGTON

Senior Lecturer, Bedford College of Higher Education

CAMBRIDGE UNIVERSITY PRESS

CAMBRIDGE

London   New York   New Rochelle
Melbourne   Sydney

Drawings by Bron of Bedford
Photographs by Tony Duffy

Published by the Press Syndicate of the University of Cambridge
The Pitt Building, Trumpington Street, Cambridge CB2 1RP
32 East 57th Street, New York, NY 10022, USA
296 Beaconsfield Parade, Middle Park, Melbourne 3206, Australia

First published 1978
Reprinted 1979, 1980

Printed in Great Britain
at the Alden Press, Oxford

Library of Congress Cataloguing in Publication Data

Elkington, Helen

Swimming

Bibliography: p.129

1. Swimming — Study and teaching. 2. Swimming
for children. I. Title.
GV837.E43 797.2'1'07 76-53514
ISBN 0 521 29027 9 paperback

Contents

Foreword

Here is a book which will give considerable step by step help to the swimming instructor. It will be of particular value to the teacher in charge of large classes of young children.

Helen Elkington knows her subject well from the teacher's viewpoint. She has had extensive experience and has not rushed into print without thoroughly testing and modifying her ideas. She has been involved in swimming at all levels from the teaching of the handicapped and absolute beginners to the training of top competitors. Knowing her experience — Helen Elkington visited Australia as a Churchill Scholar — I am prepared to vouch for the fact that her ideas on fundamental techniques will lay a firm foundation for the swimming development of the youngster. Some of Helen's teaching ideas for groups are new to me. We shall make sure that instructors in our Swim School have a copy of this book and we shall put many of these methods into practice.

Of course the aim of swimming classes should not be to force everybody into competition, although as a preparation for life this is valuable and most will enjoy it. Few would argue that ALL children should be taught to swim, and as young as is practicable. Success in international competition as well as good swimming depend on sound teaching from an early age. We hear that the East Germans plan to have all children swimming BEFORE they enter primary school, that is by 5 years of age! Then we shall need another book on what to do with the 5-year-old competent swimmer.

This handbook is sure to be widely welcomed by teachers and in the growing number of swimming schools. I believe that many courses will be based on the procedures advocated, and no doubt some modifications and additions will be made to existing systems.

Regular swimming instruction should be part of every child's education and it needs to be carried out systematically and well. Helen Elkington's book is a real contribution to the literature on swimming. It has come at the right time.

Forbes Carlile, M.Sc.
former Australian and Dutch Olympic Coach
Sydney, Australia

Preface

Swimming is an essential part of every child's physical education. This book is primarily a handbook for teachers of children up to the age of thirteen or fourteen and for student teachers. It is hoped that all who work with young children, not forgetting parents, will find it of equal value.

The teacher has the responsibility of introducing swimming to children in such a way that they will find it irresistible, challenging the imagination and calling for mental as much as physical effort. This reflects the best of today's approaches to physical education. The old static introduction to swimming is fortunately rapidly disappearing. Now children are encouraged to experience the thrill of moving in water in their first lesson in activities which are enjoyable and meaningful from the start.

Swimming must be taught with imagination and enthusiasm if the children are to respond and achieve success. The aim of this book is to provide teachers of swimming with all the practical information they will require and help them make their lessons challenging, enjoyable and effective.

Helen Elkington

Bedford, 1977

Acknowledgements

I would like to express my appreciation to the following associations, educational establishments and individuals for their contribution to my swimming experience.

The High School for Girls, Clifton, Bristol, England.
Coventry College of Education, England.
The Physical Education Association of Great Britain and Northern Ireland.
The Amateur Swimming Association, England.
The Scottish Amateur Swimming Association.
The Amateur Athletic Union of the United States, Inc.
The New Zealand Amateur Swimming Association.
The Australian Swimming Union.
The Sport Foundation of South Africa.
The Winston Churchill Memorial Trust, England.
Bedford College of Physical Education, England.
Mr Forbes and Mrs Ursula Carlile, Australia.
Mrs Wilbur Davies, England.
Mr Henry and Mrs Beulah Gundling, U.S.A.
Mr Don and Mrs Marion Kane, U.S.A.
Mr 'Bert' Kinnear, England.
Mr Kenneth Lyons, England.
Miss Pauline McCullagh, Canada.
Mrs Peg Seller, Canada.

The many other friends and colleagues in swimming too numerous to mention individually and above all the hundreds of beginners and swimmers it has been my fortune to teach or coach.

H.J.E.

1 General philosophy

THE VALUE OF SWIMMING

1   *Survival.* Everyone must be given the opportunity to become a competent swimmer. Many children and adults lose their lives in water each year. It can be such an attractive and enjoyable element for those confident in it, but it is also a dangerous environment and one to be respected. We should do our utmost to drownproof and waterproof children as soon as possible. Too many teachers feel their job has finished when the pupil has managed to swim a few yards; children are often classed as swimmers when they struggle a length of the pool. But this is only a beginning — they must be guided to improve their technique to swim better, more strongly over greater distances. Life saving should be introduced at some stage but children must know how to save *themselves* first.
2   *Fitness.* Swimming is a popular form of exercise for the able bodied and the disabled. Age is no barrier and numbers aren't important; it is as suitable for individuals as for groups. It is an ideal family activity.
3   *Fun.* Swimming is fun from the moment a learner first gets his feet off the bottom of the pool. All kinds of water sports and activities lie ahead — for some the ability to swim is essential, for others it is necessary if they are to be enjoyed fully and in safety.

INTRODUCING CHILDREN TO WATER

Parents can do much to familiarise children with water. Babies can be introduced to it by playing in the bath at home. A child of a few months will benefit tremendously from having made friends with water. By the time he reaches the nursery school or his first swimming lesson he knows what to expect. It

1

Introduction of partially sighted baby to water with mother

helps if the child's mother or father (in the early stages) introduces him to the swimming pool. A petrified child has invariably been frightened or put off earlier in life. Parents must guard against this.

It is very important for nursery, infant and primary school age children to be taken swimming. I know the problems with timetabling, expense, staffing, transport, and helpers to dress and undress the very small. Parents can often help. No child should enter senior school still a non-swimmer.

FIRST LESSONS AND ENVIRONMENT

The following points should be borne in mind.

1   The water and surrounding air temperature should be comfortable —

2

the water temperature ideally around 27°C (80° F) with the air temperature slightly higher to prevent excessive humidity.

2 There should be ample room in the pool. The *size* of the class must be considered. Classes which are too large are often noisy and can be dangerous. Many local Education Authorities stipulate a maximum class in the range of twenty to twenty-five children per teacher.

3 A lesson a day for three weeks is better than a lesson a week for fifteen weeks. Lessons at first should be short, e.g. fifteen to twenty minutes with plenty of movement.

4 The dimensions of the pool must obviously be suited to the children's age and ability. Nursery and infant children can be taught in shallow pools and many schools now have teaching pools. A shallow pool is admirable initially but once the children are swimming more depth is needed and it is worth having a pool which can be filled to one metre or so. A pool of constant depth (no deep or shallow end) is preferable.

5 The pool and all apparatus should be made as attractive as possible with bright colours. Imaginative designs on the pool walls and bottom can contribute greatly. I remember seeing a class of children in Moana swimming pool, South Island, New Zealand being set the task of touching the fish design inlaid in the tiles on the pool bottom. The colour, shape, size, and texture of apparatus all intrigue the young and add to the fun of their activities with them.

6 The pool should have a removable teaching rail.

7 Changing rooms must be warm.

8 Small children often have problems in putting their clothes on pegs and keeping them together. An excellent idea is to have the children put their clothing into shoe bags.

9 Showers, foot baths and toilets must be clean. Attitudes to hygiene and safety should be reinforced in swimming lessons. Pupils should help to maintain the cleanliness of the facilities they use and their own personal hygiene.

10 An alarm system should be available in all pools. It horrifies me that very few school pools have made adequate provision for emergencies. There must be a suitable warning device for pupils in the water (e.g. a siren or hooter), safety poles available, and quick access to a telephone.

2 General principles

Every new class should be given a code of conduct. This should cover safety, discipline and hygiene.

SAFETY AND DISCIPLINE

1   Swimmers should not enter the pool before a member of staff has given permission.
2   Swimmers should be made aware of the depth of the pool and understand diving precautions. For example, a vertical dive from the bathside should not be made into less than 2.6 metres of water. The diver should look before diving to make sure the area is clear of other people.
3   No running on the bathside.
4   No pushing in.
5   Non-swimmers should wear coloured caps to identify them. This is a particularly important consideration for teachers working in open water. (Red, yellow, luminous pink, orange, etc. are all good.)
6   Courlene rope (rope especially made to stand up to wear and tear in chlorinated and salt water) is useful for marking safe areas of the pool. Coloured cork and buoys tied to the rope are also valuable.
7   Children must respond promptly to signals. A whistle or siren can be used in dangerous situations but the children must know exactly what the signal means and what to do in emergencies.
8   Swimmers must know how to help themselves if they get cramp. They should be instructed to use the unaffected limbs and to get to the side where help is usually available. They should know what to do if help isn't available. (See personal survival skills, p. 87.)
9   No pupil should swim immediately after a meal.

10   Chewing gum is highly dangerous and should be prohibited.
11   In a public pool there must be strong swimmers or life guards to keep watch over a group.
12   All pupils should know where to obtain first aid equipment.
13   Long poles and life belts should be placed at set points and pupils instructed in their use.

The teacher must have a sound working knowledge of methods of resuscitation. (The expired air method particularly.) The teacher must also be able to swim competently and if necessary rescue and land any pupil in his charge.

IMPORTANT All teachers of swimming must have a copy of *The Royal Life Saving Society Handbook* and know it well.

HYGIENE

1   Pupils should not swim if they have any foot or skin infection.
2   They should not swim if they have a severe cold or ear trouble.
3   Outdoor shoes must not be worn on the bathside.
4   Swimming costumes should be rinsed and wrung out (*not* in the pool!) after use.
5   Pupils who have long hair should wear caps for hygiene and swimming efficiency.
6   The toilet and showers should be used before entering the pool.

THE TEACHER AND PUPIL

The swimming teacher has to teach in an extremely difficult environment, indoors and outdoors. Every effort should be made to ensure that the teacher and pupil can see one another for effective demonstrations and safety, and that the teacher can be heard.

A happy working relationship between teacher and pupil is essential. The first impression must be good. The teacher should *dress* appropriately. The teacher's *attitude* should be pleasant, with a well placed sense of humour and enthusiasm and plenty of constructive advice. The teacher's *voice* can play a crucial part. It can inspire or bore. It is essential to the relationship between teacher and pupil. Volume, enunciation, speed of delivery and expression are

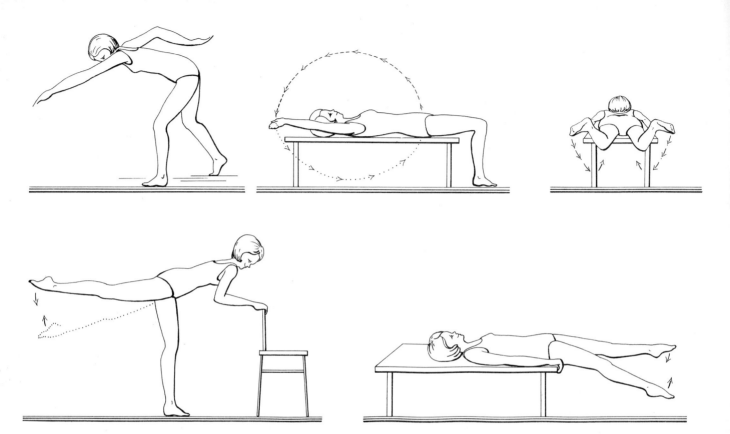

Demonstrating arm and leg action at the bathside. Note body positions

all important and should be varied to suit the situation. As well as speaking more loudly, the further a teacher is from the pupil, remember to speak more slowly. He should not talk too much and should keep sentences short and to the point. The pupils should be made to *think* with the questions, and appropriate use made of their answers.

Demonstrations by the teacher provide the visual guidance often necessary to accompany verbal description. They must be technically accurate and the teacher must be positioned on the bathside so that he can be seen and imitated by the pupils in the water. The arm action of the prone stroke should be demonstrated with the teacher bent forwards at the hips, whereas to demonstrate the supine stroke arm action, the teacher should lie on a bench at the bathside. The children should have a chance to see the demonstration from different angles — the side view of the arm action can show the length of the pull, and the forward view the width and line of the underwater stroke.

The group watching must be in a position enabling them to see, hear and practise the skills (and they should not have to look into the sun). Hand signals are often used in large pools to save shouting but the pupils should be brought together in a small group for detailed instruction.

The teacher should have a whistle and use it with discretion. The class should know that at a blast of the whistle they stop, look at the teacher and listen carefully.

EQUIPMENT

Swimming aids are invaluable and ample opportunity should be given to the pupils to experiment with them. They will create interest, excitement and movement, give confidence and generally add to the fun of the lesson.

Apparatus should be selected carefully. Consideration should be given to colour (the brighter the better), shape, texture and function. Aids should be chosen that impede movement as little as possible and that are absolutely safe. Adaptability is worth looking for: this can be particularly valuable in work with disabled children.

Aids have the following uses which the teacher should keep in mind when buying them:

1   To support swimmers *a* beginners
                          b learning new skills
                          c correcting skills and faults
2   To aid propulsion
3   To encourage breathing
4   For sectionalised practice (e.g. legs only)
5   To swim round, under, onto, through and to pick up.

Suggested aids:

Rubber rings. There are three sizes — small (16-inch) for small children, medium (18-inch) for larger children and young adults, and large (20-inch) for adults.

The rubber ring should be secured to the swimmer, so that it does not slip down to the knees. A tape running over the shoulder tied to the ring is ideal.

Arm bands. There are different sizes and some arm bands have double chambers, others single. They should have a secure stopper.

Entering water with rubber ring secured to the swimmer

Floats in open rack

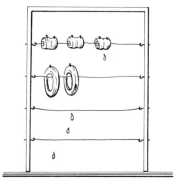

Armbands and rings on courlene rope

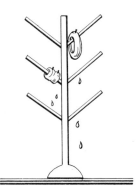

'The Christmas tree'

Some arm bands have a flat section designed to be worn on the inner side of the arm for freer movement. A double chambered arm band can be cut in half crossways to make an arm band adequate for very small children.

Floats. The most recent trend is for the float to be made of polystyrene or polystyrene foam. It's less easy for children to bite chunks from the latter! The size of the float is more important than the material however. A float about 25 cm long and 5 cm thick is to be preferred for children. Larger floats are more suitable for young adults.

Hoops and toys. Large hoola-hoops in bright red and blue are ideal for underwater activity. They can be weighted to stand in a vertical position under the surface. Balls, ducks, boats, etc. are good for pushing or blowing along the surface.

Rubber bricks. Bricks can be used for picking up from the bottom of the pool. Colour is important so that the brick can be easily seen. A brick weighing 2 kg is ideal for primary children.

Pole and noose. A broom handle with a courlene rope threaded through a hose pipe to form a loop will support the body in the prone or supine position (see diagram on p. 18).

Float suit. A girl's swimming costume with polystyrene bullet shaped floats which are placed in pockets all round the costume. The floats can be removed as necessary enabling the learner to move horizontally in the prone or supine position.

Markers. Reels of courlene rope, and also yachting buoys are invaluable for marking off pool areas, even better if they are of various colours. When children are swimming up and down the pool, for example, they can be set to swim up beside one rope and down beside another.

A clock with a sweep second hand is very useful for chain swimming, survival and speed work. A small drum to beat out rhythms is also useful.

3 The early lessons

I have already mentioned the advantage of an early introduction to water. By the time the child is six or so he is able to understand and co-ordinate movements and at an ideal age to learn the basic essentials of strokes. Remember children differ in learning ability just as they vary physically, intellectually, and emotionally. Natural ability must be allowed to develop.

One must not be dogmatic about teaching methods. The facilities available, the frequency and length of lessons and the pupils' abilities must all be taken into account. Pupils must also have ample opportunity to experiment and discover.

The teacher can give guidance in three main ways — verbally, visually and manually. In all instances the pupil must be successful if interest is to be maintained. If the pupils are in a pool which is not large the whole point of the lesson can be lost if the teacher does not organise the space properly. It is often best to divide the class into sets of two. 'Number ones' swim across the pool and when they reach halfway, 'twos' follow in the same path. 'Ones' arrive at the opposite side and pause until 'twos' arrive, and then number 'ones' return and the procedure is repeated. This prevents overcrowding and large gaps in the lesson.

FIRST STAGE

1 *The beginners' class*

A class of beginners is one of the most exciting, enjoyable and challenging experiences, an ideal class — bubbling with enthusiasm and desperate to learn. All that the children require is guidance in the skills, and progress is soon evident. A few will be apprehensive but these pupils are in the minority A lot of apparatus should be used, and in a large pool a courlene rope should mark off a safe area to ensure children do not stray out of their depth. Some children do not like the splash of others in the group and are loath to try strokes with so much water disturbance. A second rope is an advantage enclosing a small area at the very shallowest part of the pool; as confidence grows it can be removed.

Children should work away from the rail in the early lessons and try things for *themselves.* The value of partner support work is questionable at this stage, particularly one beginner supporting another, because (*a*) it wastes the time of one child, (*b*) the supporting partner gets cold and (*c*) the support is invariably incorrect and confidence can be lost.

The following approach is successful and *a–f* are progressions which can be attempted in the first lesson and repeated in the following two or three.

a   *Before the lesson* make sure each child has a suitable size rubber ring with a safety tape running over the shoulder, and arm bands. Spread the children out on the bathside and get them to stretch their arms sideways, eyes looking upwards and bending the knees. This is important; it shows the children how to space themselves out and bend their knees because, once in the water, their shoulders must be underneath to help general stability, with the arms stretched sideways for balance and the eyes looking upwards to prevent toppling forwards.

b   *Entry* can be by the steps (see page 7) or from a sitting position on the bathside. For the second method the pupil stretches across the body, placing both hands on the bathside and pressing them firmly downwards, and swivels round to lower himself into the water.

c   *Movement.* The children bend their knees, shoulders under water, arms stretched sideways, eyes looking upwards. They weave in and out of one another using all the space available. They should experiment with their feet moving forwards, backwards and sideways. This enables them to discover how to transfer their weight in order to move efficiently — moving forwards from heel to toe, or back from toe to heel, or sidestepping. The size of the steps can vary. 'What size steps help you to move quickly?' As the children move, the teacher should encourage them to put their faces in the water. 'You have a black spot on your nose, draw large patterns in the water — circles, squares, triangles.' A drum can be most effective at this stage — the children move in time to the beat and change direction on a heavier beat. I find this is most successful at getting children involved and overcoming any reservations they might have. Music with a good rhythm is also useful. Coloured

Sit and swivel entry

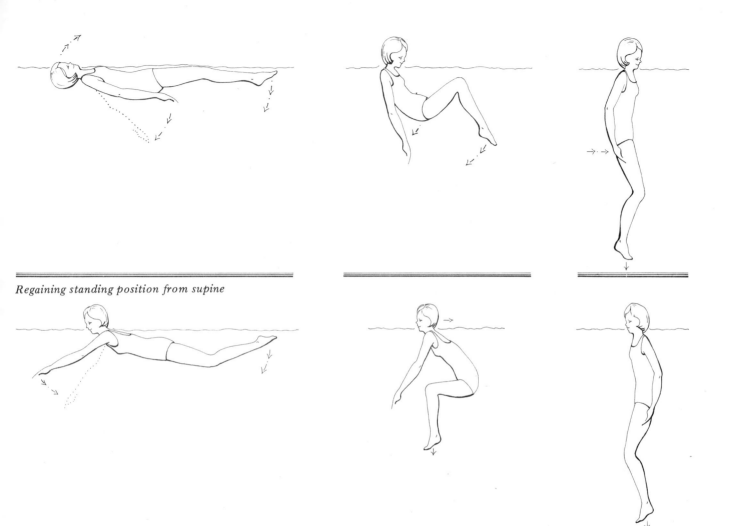

Regaining standing position from supine

Regaining standing position from prone

balls are good for interest too. The children blow or push them along with their noses, head, or hands. Their feet will begin to lift slightly from the pool bottom.

d   *Buoyancy.* The children must be able to float on their fronts (prone) and on their backs (supine), roll over, and stand up. They spread their arms wide, look upwards and imagine they are going to sit down. As they do this they discover both feet lifting off the bottom. Repeat this several times.

11

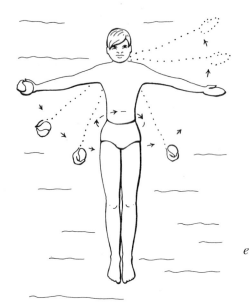

Learning to roll around the longtitudinal axis using a ball: the right arm remains in the water and stretches across the body to place the ball in the left hand

The children should now be shown how to plant their feet firmly back on the bottom if they are launched onto their fronts or backs.

The pupils should be taught to roll from their backs to their fronts and vice versa.

Children respond very well through their imagination. 'Think of a piece of toast. You are going to make yourselves as brown as you can.' They usually stretch their arms and legs, wide and they are floating! 'Try to get both sides toasted.' 'One small part of you only is going to get toasted — make yourselves smaller.' This brings a tuck shape or a thin narrow shape. The teacher can thus bring about a useful transfer between the three common shapes, i.e. wide/wall, narrow/pin, tuck/ball. Finally 'Who can get toasted on one side and roll over and get toasted on the other side?'

e *Propulsion.* There is no reason why pupils with rings and arm bands should not experiment with arm actions and discover how to pull themselves through the water. They will either use a dog paddle — a long pull with alternate arms starting in an extended position in front of their faces and pulling right through to touch the hips or, still on the front, a simultaneous movement with hands and arms held firmly to push the water aside, like swimming through long grass or thick mud. Let them blow out as they move about. This prevents the 'blue' faces and bursting cheeks common to all non-swimmers trying desperately to concentrate on their new skills.

A kick can be added to the dog paddle arm action but the breast-stroke kick should be taught carefully before co-ordinating it with simultaneous arm action.

Some children love kicking alternately on their backs which is fine

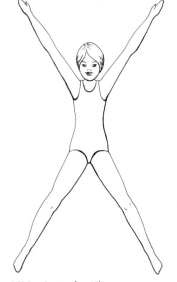

Wide shape (wall)

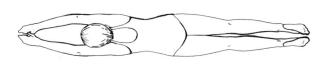

Thin shape (pin)

Tuck shape (ball)

as they are learning the first stage of an attractive stroke in which breathing is very much easier.

f *Submerging.* The pupils vary in their reaction to underwater activity. Rings must be removed and usually arm bands.

Weighted hoops are placed in different areas of the shallow end. 'Find different ways of getting through your hoop — head first, feet first, sideways', etc. Bricks and flippers can be picked up from the pool bottom. If the child finds difficulty in sinking, experiment with *speed* of submerging, i.e. 'Tuck up and sit quickly and blow out as you do so.' Or the teacher can hold a pole at the poolside for the pupil to climb down hand over hand.

'Which part of your body can you rest on the bottom of the pool?' (Head, seat, knees, hands, feet, hip, tummy, back, etc.) 'Run round to the drum beat, on every heavy beat sit on the bottom of the pool.'

Picking up objects from pool bottom

Lifting timid pupil into the pool

2 *The timid pupil*

The timid pupil requires individual help and it is usually necessary to help him at a time when the pool is quiet, generally outside lesson times. Once the pupil has experienced some success, fear will begin to go and more adventurous tasks can be attempted until he can eventually participate in a class lesson. The teacher can instill confidence in any timid non-swimmer by support given manually and by appropriate verbal encouragement.

Possible activities with the pupil wearing a rubber ring and armbands are these:

a *Entry.* The teacher enters the water first via the steps demonstrating how to enter correctly (turning at the top of the steps with the back to the pool, and looking down to see the feet are firmly placed) *or* enters the water and lifts the pupil into the pool.

b   The teacher holds the pupil firmly as illustrated in the diagram. The teacher's and pupil's shoulders should be under water and the pupil should slide his feet along the pool bottom to get the feel of movement. After this the feet should be lifted and pressed firmly back on the bottom of the pool. The pupil should be asked simple questions — 'Which part of your foot do you put on the ground?' and encouraged to walk forwards — backwards — sideways.

c   The teacher alters the support. The pupil extends the arms sideways, and looks upwards. Both feet should be lifted a few inches off the pool bottom and then replaced. This should be repeated several times. The support of the teacher should be removed and the pupil should try the task unsupported. Can the knees be tucked to the chest?

d   The teacher should show the pupil how to launch onto the front or back, stand up or roll over in the water. No pupil will feel secure until he can do these things. The pupil will be doing well and feel happier. The teacher, talking gently, should encourage a kick on the front and back now.

e   Use a coloured ball and encourage the pupil to push it along with the hands, nose or head. This is a real achievement as the pupil will be working without support.

f   The lesson could conclude with the pupil lying in a floating star shape position on his back in the water. Can he change to a thinner or tucked shape?

Teacher supporting pupil

Teacher showing the pupil how to kick on front and back

15

The timid child's individual lesson should be short but full of variety. (I would suggest ten to fifteen minutes.)

With patience and understanding from the teacher success will follow. The timid pupil should then progress to the activities suggested for the beginners' class.

SECOND STAGE

The children are now ready to progress to a more advanced stage and the following are some possibilities:

1 *The multi-stroke artificial aid lesson*

Teachers should not impose their favourite stroke on the children. There has been success in the earlier lessons and interest must be maintained. It can be very disheartening if a child is forced to work on a stroke which he is physically unable to cope with; for example not every child can cope with breaststroke which requires flexible ankles.

The multi-stroke artificial aid approach is educationally sound. The pupils wear rings, arm bands and hold floats. The leg action of the four main strokes, i.e. front and back crawl, breaststroke and dolphin butterfly stroke, can be introduced. The children experiment and discover for themselves the kick most suited to them. They can then proceed to work on their kick and breathing, and remove aids and progress to arm strokes as confidence grows.

2 *The shallow water method*

This method can be used with infant or primary age children. The pool needs to be 30–45 cm *constant* depth. The pupil can then move around on the front or back using hands on the pool bottom to propel, balance and support him. Artificial aids need not be used.

3 *The flipper float method*

This is a suitable method for individual tuition. The pupil lies in the prone or supine position with a rubber ring, armbands, flippers and holding one or two floats. The stretched position can be achieved with the support of a large

Working on leg action using floats

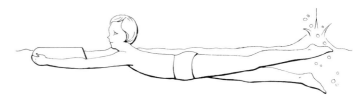

Front crawl using two floats

Front crawl using one float

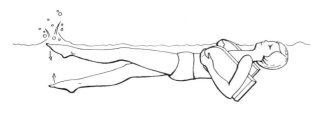

Back crawl with two floats

Back crawl with one float

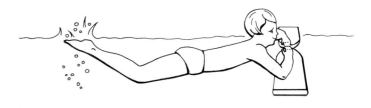

Breaststroke with two floats

Dolphin stroke with two floats

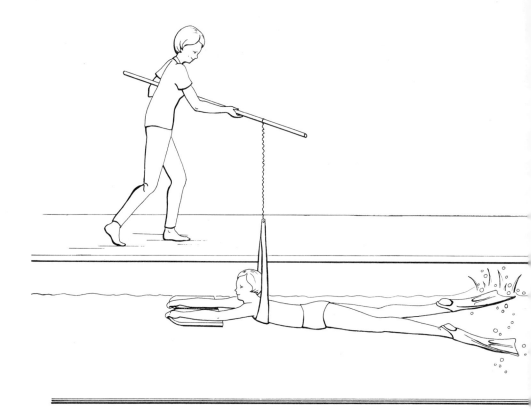

noose suspended on a broom handle held by the teacher. The noose should be placed under the armpits of the prone swimmer and under the shoulder blades or the back of the neck for a swimmer on his back. The swimmer kicks and as confidence grows the noose can be lowered. With the aid of the flippers the swimmer travels rapidly forwards no longer requiring the extra support.

This is not an ideal method for an infant or primary school class, but while most of the children are learning by one of the other methods one or two individuals might benefit from the flipper float method to get them moving initially. If a pupil tends to over bend the knees when kicking, flippers also often help to straighten the leg and encourage a swing from the hip.

4 Whole — part — whole method

Many new skills are learnt easily by the whole — part — whole approach. In this method the pupils are first shown the *whole* stroke they are about to work on. Basic guidance is given by the teacher and the pupils then try for themselves. Their efforts will probably initially appear very rough, but the idea is for the pupils to feel the whole movement and rhythm of the stroke. They then progress to *part* practice with the stroke broken down into sections, e.g. leg action, arm action, or arm action and breathing co-ordinated. The pupil finally returns to the *whole* stroke and, hopefully, improvement is evident.

The whole — part — whole approach is favoured by many. My preference is to build a stroke on a sound leg kick as in the initial stages the kick can greatly affect the body position, stability, propulsion and general rhythm.

GAME ACTIVITIES

'Play with a purpose' is an ideal method of getting used to water. Activities can be under water and on the surface, and if they are made challenging and exciting the children will progress in many ways.

The children move in time to a drum beat

It is important to ensure the children are happy in water by working along the lines I have mentioned, *before* 'regimenting' them into several weeks of work on specific strokes. But they should eventually be taught the correct way to swim each stroke once they have experienced the thrill of water as a medium to move in. The following are some suggestions for games.

Under water (Aids should be removed for underwater games.)

a   Weighted hoops, bricks, coffee jar tops and flippers can be picked up from the bottom of the pool.

b   Certain objects can be used to swim through, round and onto, e.g. hoops, weighted skittles and mats.

c   A very effective game is to get the children to swim or walk and, at a whistle or drum beat, submerge and pick up an object. I have tried this to music too and it is even more exciting for the children. It works like musical chairs. When the music stops the children submerge.

d   'Who can stand on their hands?' 'Who can kneel?' 'Who can sit?' This will encourage many children to submerge and the teacher keeps them moving by telling them to move from one part of the pool to another before surfacing.

e   Swimming underwater (for those able to swim) individually. 'How many ways can you find of swimming underwater?' 'What helps to keep you down as you swim?'

f   'Pretend you are making a cup of tea underwater.'

Above water (Aids can be used.)

a   Blowing, nosing or heading objects across the width of the pool.

b   Blowing a ball across the width and round floating objects, e.g. buoys.

c   Scull across the pool (sculling is described below) on the back with a float resting on the tummy.

d   An egg and spoon race using table tennis balls.

e   Pushing a float to the opposite side of the pool or swimming round a buoy or an object to return to the starting side.

f   'Mr Shark'. The class all spread out behind a leader and start walking across the pool behind him. The children keep saying 'What's the time, Mr Shark?' and the leader gives a time. The children go on until his

Blowing ball along

reply is 'Dinnertime!'. Then they have to turn tail and reach the pool side before they are touched.

g   Ropes can be useful. The children can follow a leader, pulling themselves across the pool. This is a particularly useful activity for some disabled swimmers.

SCULLING

Sculling is an important skill which can be used in association with the back crawl leg action, the inverted breaststroke kick or in learning watermanship generally. It is included in the stroke section because of its value with the leg actions mentioned.

Sculling can propel, balance and control the body. The hands move inwards and outwards at the wrists. In the head first or standard scull, the pattern of the hand movement is similar to a figure of eight (i.e. on the outward

21

1. Standard or head first scull

2. Reverse or foot first scull

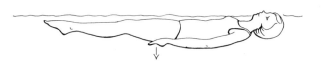

3. Stationary or flat scull

1.

2.

3.

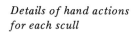

Details of hand actions for each scull

movement the thumb draws the first half of the figure of eight and on the inward movement the little finger draws the second half). In all sculling the hands are kept flat, with the fingers together and stretched. The force is applied in the direction opposite to the direction of travel. The more continuous the force the better, and the faster the sculling action the greater the force.

There are numerous sculls but the three main sculls are probably the most useful to the primary teacher.

1   Standard or head first scull.
2   Reverse or foot first scull.
3   Stationary or flat scull.

Teaching points for sculling:

1   The elbows should be as straight as possible during the sculling movements. The arms should be close to the body.

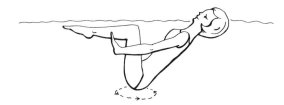

Starting and finishing position   *The tub*

2   The hand position needs to be constantly adjusted to maintain pressure. A firm flat hand with fingers together is essential.

3   Smooth continuous pivoting from the wrists will aid steady travel and propulsion.

4   The speed of sculling can help propulsion and the body position. In a firm speedy scull the body should stay flat and travel smoothly. Efficiency in sculling provides great scope, making movement more enjoyable and encouraging freer use of the pool area.

Activities:

Sculling can be improved by practice. Sculling to a drum beat will maintain interest.

1   Sculling to a drum beat head first, on the spot, feet first. Changing scull every time there is a *heavy* drum beat.

2   Sculling to music. Change direction of the scull as the phrasing of the music suggests. 'Side Saddle' is an excellent piece of music to scull to.

Stunts (Children have to be quite proficient to cope with these):

Gymnastic skills are often termed 'stunts'. Stunts can be simple or advanced and should be fun. In them the arms are used to propel, balance, turn, spin and control. Teachers can experiment and invent their own stunts or encourage the children to invent their own. Here are three:

1   *Tub.* Start with the body stationary in the supine position. The flat scull should be used. The head is kept steady, eyes looking upwards

Somersault back tuck

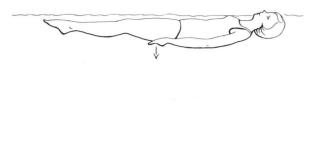

Starting and finishing positions   *Compact ball shape*

with the legs and feet extended and together. The arms are by the side sculling (this is called the back layout position). The knees are drawn towards the chest, with knees and feet in line with the water surface until the thighs are vertical.

Once the pupil is in the tub position with the eyes still looking upwards, he should revolve smoothly through 360° in a clockwise direction with the seat acting as a pivot point.

The sculling action is important for balance and control. Remember that to rotate clockwise the right hand should be used in a standard scull and the left hand in reverse.

2 *Somersault back tuck* (No rubber ring should be worn during this stunt.) Start with the body in an extended position on the back. The knees are drawn towards the chest and the head is tucked in making a very compact ball shape. The body rotates backwards in the ball shape as the arms sweep forwards. The somersault should be performed *near* the water surface. A teacher should not have to look eight feet down to find his pupils somersaulting.

3 *Log Roll.* Start in the back horizontal layout position, arms stretched beyond the head. Maintain the stretched position; the thumbs can be locked and the legs and feet should be close together. The pupil rolls at the surface about his longitudinal axis. Once the roll has been achieved the number of rolls and speed can be increased.

I usually say 'Lie on your back, stretch your arms beyond your head and glue your feet together — now imagine you are a pancake and keep that stretched position, without kicking, roll over onto your tummy

Log roll

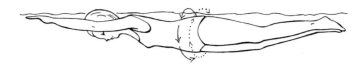

Starting and finishing position from above

An arm band round one or both ankles can help lift the feet to the surface. This is useful with heavy limbed pupils. It is not ideal for beginners or small children. This method must only be used under careful supervision.

and then onto your back again.' Some will manage with tremendous piking and the odd little kick! Once the children have tried, help them further. Show them a stretched position, arms extended beyond the head, thumbs locked and legs and feet stretched and together. Then show them how to start rolling, e.g. to roll to the right. 'Glue your right ear to your right arm, stretch your right side a little more than your left side, pike your hips a little and then push your hips to the left.' This will start the body roll to the right.

4 Lesson planning and organisation

Initially a beginners' class can be taught as *one* group. Individuals begin to develop and progress at different rates. The *mixed ability* class emerges. To an inexperienced teacher this can present a problem. The lesson must be challenging and fun for the whole class. The three main considerations are (*a*) selecting appropriate material, (*b*) planning the lesson according to time and facilities available and (*c*) organising the class for the activities.

Lessons should flow and they must not be fragmentary. Many teachers would be surprised if they timed a class and realised how much less movement there is in a lesson than they think. If a specific number of widths is set (six widths dog paddle for example) the more able swimmers will finish before the less able. There will be gaps, boredom, loss of interest and possibly misbehaviour. It is far wiser for the teacher to give the pupils *one* teaching point to concentrate on and set them off saying 'Off you go', then move up and down the poolside helping the swimmers individually. The only occasion when a specific number of widths can be set satisfactorily is in a scheduled or timed distance swim.

Pupil demonstration can lead to a halt in the lesson, but can be invaluable if the demonstration can be seen by the whole class. In most instances the class should get onto the bathside so that they can see properly, and a commentary should cover the points the teacher wishes to emphasise. It is vital for the pupils to 'have a go' themselves immediately after a demonstration.

SELECTION OF APPROPRIATE MATERIAL

The following are the main considerations:
a   Age of pupils.
b   Ability of pupils.

c   Time available.

d   Temperature and conditions generally in and out of the pool.

The material for a very young class might well be mainly confidence building activities with plenty of movement both above and under water and the opportunity to experiment with and without apparatus. The material for older more able children might combine confidence and watermanship skills and attention to certain parts of a stroke. For children more advanced still the lesson might cover watermanship, stroke work, diving or survival skills.

On pages 28–35 I have tabulated material which might be suitable for children of various abilities in specimen lesson plans.

ORGANISATION OF THE CLASS FOR THE ACTIVITIES

The length, width and depth of pool must be carefully considered. Small pools may pose a problem. The following pool plans are suggested. The teacher should experiment with the ideal for his pool.

Courlene rope is essential and can be tied or hooked to the rail. If there is no rail, brackets can be made to hook into the trough or edge of the bath surround. The rope can divide the pool lengthways or widthways. A clock with a second hand is also useful.

PLANNING THE LESSON FOR THE TIME AND FACILITIES AVAILABLE

Teachers' lesson plans may vary in layout, but the aim is usually the same. Tasks in the lesson can be subjective, objective or both. A subjective task concentrates on technique, whereas an objective activity is usually one designed to measure ability against time or distance. Technique in the latter case is not the most important consideration.

The lesson can be set out with an introduction, followed by the main theme — 'the meaty' part of the lesson, a conclusion, and finally a contrasting activity. The teacher should ensure that the lesson is balanced. If, in the teaching of a skill, part of the lesson has been a little static, the next part should be very active.

The introduction should be planned to attract attention, interest the class and introduce the main aim of the lesson. The introduction may also need to

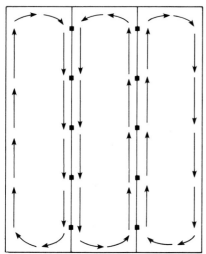

Similar ability group
Chain swimming.
Lanes 1 and 3 swim clockwise. Lane 2 swims anticlockwise. Space the swimmers a few yards apart in each lane for a time distance swim – 'see how far you can swim in three minutes'.

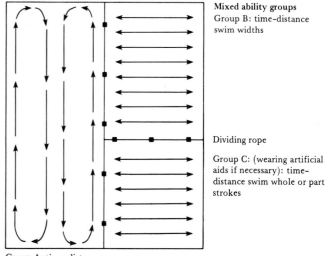

Mixed ability groups
Group B: time–distance swim widths

Dividing rope

Group C: (wearing artificial aids if necessary): time–distance swim whole or part strokes

Group A: time–distance swim lengths

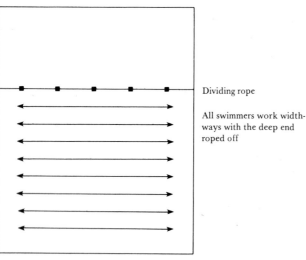

Dividing rope

All swimmers work widthways with the deep end roped off

An intermediate standard group

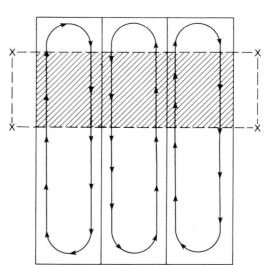

Similar ability group
The swimmers do a head first surface dive within this area as they swim towards the deep end, and a foot first dive as they swim towards the shallow end.

A time–distance swim including a head first and foot first surface dive. (This is a suitable task for a small group.)

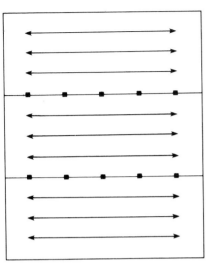

Mixed ability groups

A: better swimmers working
widthways on whole
stroke work

Dividing rope

B: average swimmers work-
ing widthways on whole
stroke and legs only
work

Dividing rope

C: weak swimmers working
widthways on multi-
stroke artificial aid
activities

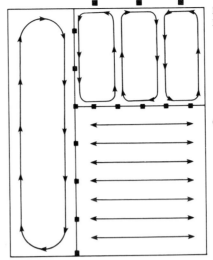

Mixed ability groups

B: intermediate swimmers
alternating laps of whole
stroke and legs only with
aids

C: weak swimmers working
on multistroke artificial
aid activities

A: chain swimming
lengths working
on whole stroke

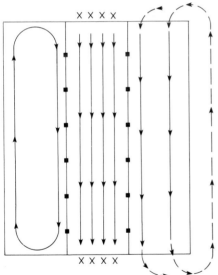

C: Weaker swim-
mers divided
into two
groups chain-
swim one
length best
stroke, get
out, *walk* to
starting end
and repeat

Mixed ability groups

A: 'Medley'.   B: Average swim-
Change stroke   mers swimming
after each lap   lengths four to
   a lane. Fastest
   swimmers go
   first followed
   by others at

three-second
intervals. Re-
peat from op-
posite end

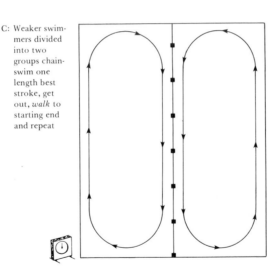

Similar ability groups

Two 'chains' swimming lengths. Swimmers start
at three-second intervals working on whole strokes
or legs only (with or without aids). Rest between
each lap.

Similar ability groups
A: diving and survival skills

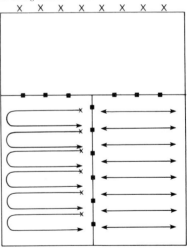

B: turns   C: sculling and waterman-
         ship

Groups should change round either within one
lesson or in successive lessons

29

be *active*, for instance if the class appears to be apathetic or if it is cold. The introduction can be verbal, a demonstration by a more able pupil or a class activity or a combination of these. But it must stimulate.

The main theme shapes the main part of the lesson when new skills are introduced or reinforced. The activities should be planned carefully to achieve this.

The conclusion is a tidying up of the lesson theme with opportunity for demonstrations by successful pupils. All pupils should then have another try.

The contrasting activity is an opportunity to introduce another aspect of swimming and can help to maintain a lively interest to the very end of the lesson. For example if the pupils have been working on strokes during the main part of the lesson, diving might be introduced in the contrasting final section.

AFTER THE LESSON

The teacher must have keen powers of observation and carefully appraise what the lesson has achieved, or failed to achieve — for the class as a whole and the individuals in it. Was the aim of the lesson achieved? Did all the children enjoy it? Was the lesson well balanced? What will the next lesson be?

SPECIMEN LESSONS

The following lesson plans are suggested themes suitable for primary classes. They also show how the lesson card can be laid out.

Example 1:
Non-swimmers/beginners
Number of pupils: 20   Time available 20 minutes

Equipment   Rings, arm bands, rubber balls, plastic hoola-hoops, drum, record: *Popcorn*, track used 'Song of the Narobi Trio'.

Details of pool   Temperature 27°C (80°F), Depth 0.75–2.5 metres, Length 25 metres, Width 12 metres.

Previous knowledge   The children have just been introduced to water and are non-swimmers.

Aim of the lesson	\multicolumn{3}{l}{To build up confidence in water. (The children all wearing rings and arm bands at this point.)}

	Time (approximate guide)	Content	Teaching points
Introductory activity	3 minutes	1 *a* Entry via the steps. *or*	At the top of the steps turn with your back to the pool.
		b Entry via the side.	Sitting, legs dangling over the bath-side. Reach across the body with the right or left hand. Both hands pressed firmly into poolside, swivel and lower yourself into the pool.
		c Standing with legs spread out, rocking from one foot to the other (weight transition).	Arms wide for balance, shoulders under water. Eyes looking upwards, legs astride — forwards and back. Rock on to the toe and then back on to the heel. Repeat this, legs astride sideways. Rock onto the feet from one side to the other.
Main theme	12–15 minutes	2 *a* Walking covering area. Experiment with large and small steps (speed).	Arms wide. Shoulders under water. Eyes look upwards. 'What size step helps you to travel fast?' 'What size steps enable you to travel slower?'
		b Noses in the water, drawing patterns with the nose.	Imagine you have a spot of paint on your nose. Draw *large* patterns, e.g. circles, squares, triangles. Move around the pool shoulders under the water.
		c Covering a large area moving in different directions to a drum beat.	Moving with shoulders under water forwards, backwards, sideways and turn. Keeping to the drum beat, i.e. change direction on the heavy beat.
		d Using a ball — push it along with the head, nose or blow it along.	Cover a large area.
		e Buoyancy activities. Sun-bathe in the water. Wide, narrow and tuck shapes in the supine and prone position.	Work on the clarity of the shape. Moving gently and smoothly from one shape to another. Try first on the back then on the front, and then roll from the back to the front.

31

Time	Content	Teaching points
	f Lying in the prone position legs together. Using the arms to pull the body along.	1 Using your arms pull yourself along like a large dog. Fingers together, hold the water, long pull, paddle action, 2 Using both arms together sweep the water backwards. 3 Choose your favourite way of using your arms and continue.

	Time	Content	Teaching points
Conclusion	2 minutes	3 *a* Sitting in a tucked position — Tub.	Imagine you are sitting in a honey pot. Travel round in the tucked position using your arms only. Forwards, sideways and backwards. Repeat to a drum beat.
Contrasting activity	3 minutes	4 *a* Using gaily coloured weighted hoops. (Children remove rubber rings.) *or* (Rings can be kept on for this activity.)	Find different ways of getting through the hoops, i.e. forwards, backwards, sideways. Which part of your body leads the way, e.g. head, feet, side, back?
		b All spread out bobbing up and down in time to music.	Shoulders under water. Arms wide for balance. Bobbing under in time to the beat.

Example 2: illustrates an orthodox lesson for a class of equal ability. The lesson concentrates on specific technical points related to a stroke, i.e. the back crawl leg action.

Back crawl

Number of pupils: 20   Time available: 15 minutes

Equipment	Floats and, for some of the weaker pupils, arm bands.
Details of pool	Temperature 27°C (80°F), Depth 0.75–2.5 metres, Length 25 metres, Width 12 metres.
Previous knowledge	The pupils have already been introduced to the front crawl and breaststroke leg kicks.
Aim of the lesson	To introduce the back crawl leg action to the class.

	Time (approximate guide)	Content	Teaching points
Introductory activity	2 minutes	1 Push, and glide on the back and stand up.	1 Holding rail or trough with two hands shoulder width apart. Feet apart and on wall.

Time	Content	Teaching points
		2 The distance covered with the drive from the wall.
		3 The shape of the body. Long and thin.
		4 Standing up: head forwards, hips sit, arms pull back strongly and turn and sweep forwards.

	Time	Content	Teaching points
Main theme	8 minutes	2 *a* Teacher demonstration of the back crawl leg kick.	1 Swing from the hips. 2 Legs stretched, toes pointed. 3 Toes break the surface of water. 4 Rhythm of the kick.
		b Pupils try the leg action holding two floats, one float under each arm.	Points of 2*a* with a check that floats are held correctly.
		c The leg action holding one float.	Points for 2*a* plus holding the one float tightly to the chest.
		d The leg action with sculling.	Leg action points as mentioned in 2*a*. Sculling — elbows straight and arms close to the side. Hands pivot from the wrist. The fingers are kept together and stretched. The force is applied at right angles to the direction of travel. Continuous rhythm is important.
Conclusion	2 minutes	3 Select a point from 2*b*, *c*, or *d* to work on and improve.	Choose the relevant points to work on.
Contrasting activity	3 minutes	4 Different body parts touching the bottom of the pool.	Rest your body on the pool bottom. Which part is taking your weight? Find another part, etc.

Example 3: illustrates an orthodox lesson for a class of mixed ability. The lesson illustrates setting specific tasks varied to meet the needs of three ability groups.

Front crawl

Number of pupils: 25   5 beginners C group, 10 mediocre swimmers B group, 10 advanced swimmers A group   Time available: 20 minutes

Equipment   Floats and, for some of the weaker pupils, rings, arm bands.

Details of pool   Temperature 27°C (80°F), Depth 0.75–2.5 metres, Length 25 metres, Width 12 metres.

	Time (approximate guide)	Content	Teaching points
Previous knowledge		All pupils have been introduced to the basic skills of the strokes but some are more advanced than others.	
Aim of the lesson		To teach new skills and improve the front crawl stroke.	

	Time (approximate guide)	Content	Teaching points
		A, B and C groups	
Introductory activity	3 minutes	1 *a* The swimmers work widthways on their favourite stroke.	Concentrating on the *rhythm* of the stroke chosen, i.e. front and back crawl and dolphin butterfly swimmers strive for continuity of the arm action. Breaststroke swimmers work for a slight glide following the kick.
		C group	
Main theme	10 minutes	2 *a* Leg kick holding a float.	1 Correct grip of the float. Swing from the hips. 2 Legs stretched. 3 Toes pointed. 4 Heels break the surface of the water. 5 Rhythm of the kick.
		b Leg kick and arms extended, i.e. thumbs locked.	Points as for 2*a* and encourage breathing.
		c Dog paddle.	1 The dog paddle — keep the arms alternating. 2 Check the grip of the water. 3 Pull right to the hip. 4 Rhythm.
		d Front crawl stroke nose in the water, holding the breath.	1 Check the flow of the arm action over the water. 2 Steadiness of head and flow of arm action.
		B group	
		2 *a* Dog paddle.	Points as for C group 2*c*.
		b Nose in the water front crawl, one breath taken halfway across the pool.	1 Steady head. 2 Flow of arm action. 3 One steady breath taken. 4 General rhythm.

Time	Content	Teaching points
	c Nose in the water front crawl, two breaths taken halfway across the pool.	Points as above.
	d Front crawl, breathing alternately.	
	A group	
	2 *a* Front crawl, breathing alternately (every other stroke cycle).	Smooth rhythm of stroke and breathing.
	b Leg kick, arms extended.	
	c Front crawl, unilateral breathing (breathing to one side).	Points as for 2*a*.
	d Front crawl, bilateral breathing (a breath is taken on alternate sides of the body every one-and-a-half stroke cycles).	Steady rhythm generally.
	A, B and C groups	
Conclusion 2 minutes	3 *a* Working on point 2*d* of each appropriate group.	
	A, B and C groups	
Contrasting activity 5 minutes	4 *a* Tucked somersaults, front and back.	1 Compact body. Nose to knees.
		2 Scull sweeps in the opposite direction to the somersault.
	b Sculling: head first	1 Sculling action (head first). Hands close to side, fingers together, flat, and raised *upwards*. Pivot at the wrist rhythmically — pushing towards the feet. The elbows should be straight.
	feet first	2 Sculling action (feet first). Repeat teaching points above but the finger tips should be downwards and pressure of the scull towards the head.

INFANT/PRIMARY SCHOOL SWIMMING PROGRAMME

At this point it is worth considering the syllabus as a whole. Remember that all lessons should be challenging, progressive, full of activity and fun.

Non-swimmers and beginners

Progressive list:

1	Safety and hygiene rules	
2	Equipment	Care of equipment. Use of equipment.

First stage

3	Early confidence activities	Entry via steps and side.
	Moving	Weight transference, patterns, direction, speed.
	Launching	onto the back and front.
	Standing up	from prone and supine.
	Buoyancy	Wide — narrow — tuck (mushroom float).
	Rotation	from front to back and vice versa.
	Propulsion	Arm actions alternating/simultaneous.
	Breathing	Blow objects along as they swim (colourful balls, ducks, etc.).
	Submerging	through objects, e.g. hoops. Body weight on pool bottom.

N.B. Use a drum beat for moving and submerging.

Second stage

4	*a*	Multi-stroke/artificial aid method	Experiment with the four main stroke leg kicks and where applicable add a paddle or scull to accompany kick. Develop favourite kick. Breathing still considered.
	b	Flipper float method	For individuals — this method can be used in conjunction with multi-stroke/artificial aid.
	c	Shallow water method	Where space and depth allow for this method.
5		Drownproofing techniques	In shallow water at this stage. The four stages: resting, getting ready, the exhale and inhale, resting.
6		Sculling	Head first, feet first, on the spot.
7		Water games	
8		Simple stunt	Tub.

Intermediate swimmers

1	Entry	Sitting dives, kneeling dives, lunge dives.

2	The swimming strokes	The basic techniques of the three main strokes and the leg actions of dolphin and inverted breaststroke. (Work on co-ordination of legs, arms and breathing.) Appreciation of stroke counting.

N.B. Encourage shorter distances with a good technique rather than longer distances with poor technique.

3	Organisation	Chain swimming and lane discipline can be introduced.
4	Drownproofing	Progress to deeper water.
5	Stunts	Log roll, tub, somersaults tucked.
6	Sculling	continued, improve technique.
7	Submerging	through hoops, pick up 4-lb brick.

Advanced swimmers

1	Entry	Crouch dive, plain header, racing start and pivot turn.
2	The swimming strokes	The improvement of the four main strokes. (N.B. Dolphin leg kick and breaststroke arm action — some very advanced top primary children could attempt the overwater recovery.)
		The inverted breaststroke kick.
3	Survival	Personal survival skills and sequence life saving for the more able.
4	Drownproofing	Continue the skills.
5	Stunts	Sequence work to include sculling and stunts to music.
6	Ball games	
7	Awards	

GENERAL INTEREST

From the start suitable well illustrated books about swimming should be available. The teachers should make use of film and film loops, charts and other visual aids. Photographs from newspapers and magazines should be collected and displayed. The children could also be encouraged to make their own scrapbooks.

5 Buoyancy and drownproofing

BUOYANCY

Many people rashly say 'I'm a sinker'. In fact very few people have nil buoyancy. They probably mean if they lie on their backs in water they sink and therefore should be classified as sinkers. There is a very simple float called the mushroom float which is an accurate method of assessing if you have a sinker in your class.

The pupil should get into the mushroom float position as illustrated, take a deep breath *in* and hold it. The body should float if the pupil has any buoyancy. If he repeats this basic test and this time blows *out,* the results are very revealing. This experience helps children appreciate the value of air in the lungs to aid flotation. (A swimmer always has some air in his lungs and can decrease his overall specific gravity by taking in more air or increase it by exhaling.)

The shape of the pupil's body can make a difference too — is he fat,

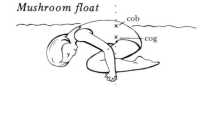

Mushroom float

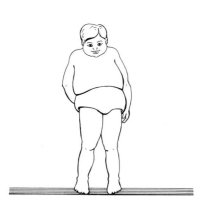

Endomorph (fat)

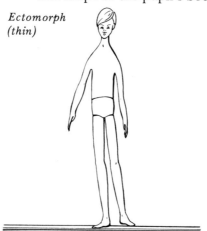

Ectomorph (thin)

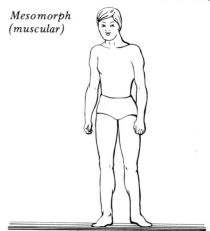

Mesomorph (muscular)

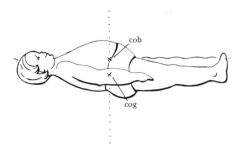

Horizontal float

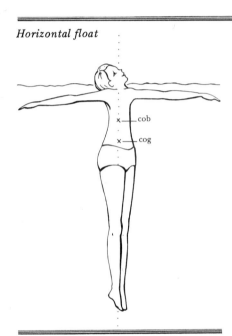

Vertical float

(*Centre of buoyancy* — cob
Centre of gravity — cog)

thin or muscular? These different body shapes will float differently. A fatter person can usually float all day on his back in a horizontal position, whereas a muscular person with not so much fat around the hip region but possibly heavy in the hips and legs will be better in deeper water — floating with arms stretched sideways and legs hanging downwards vertically. The angle of flotation depends upon the relation between the centre of buoyancy (fat and air) and the centre of gravity (bone and muscle). The human body usually has a specific gravity a little below 1.00 and this enables most people to swim with most of the body in the water.

Adjusting the position of the limbs and head can help too — if a swimmer in the supine position places his arms by his side he may find his feet sinking; transferring the arms beyond the head has a balancing effect, because weight transferred beyond the head will generally lift the feet. Beginners should experiment with body positions to find the ideal one for floating, e.g. wide, narrow or tucked.

The water the swimmer is immersed in can affect buoyancy too. The specific gravity of fresh water is 1.00. The human body, as already mentioned, usually has a specific gravity a little less than 1.00 and can usually float even in fresh water. Salt water has a slightly higher specific gravity and is far easier for everyone to float in. If water is warmed appreciably the specific gravity is a little lower. In top level competitive swimming the temperature of the water is carefully checked, therefore.

Points for the teacher to consider

1   *The body*
    Density of the body relative to the water (its specific gravity).
    Body type: fat, thin or muscular.
    The position of the centre of gravity (bone and muscle), and centre of buoyancy (fat and air).
    Distribution of body weight and shape.
    The amount of air in the lungs.
    CAN THE PUPIL MUSHROOM FLOAT?

2   *The water*
    The specific gravity of the water — salt or fresh?

A lesson on buoyancy can be invaluable. Pupils should experiment with floating in various positions.

DROWNPROOFING

Drownproofing is a set of simple skills for survival in an emergency. It is also a good watermanship activity for beginners. It has a value in showing pupils the need to conserve energy in an emergency by remaining on the spot and surviving with as little movement as possible. It relies on efficiency in breathing and confidence under water. A drownproofed pupil should have the ability to remain on the spot in the water for an indefinite length of time.

In the early 1960s attention in this country was drawn to Fred Lanoue's book: *Drownproofing*. The technique I am describing is a simplified form I find successful with younger children. I show pupils the four main stages of the technique in the shallow end and they go on to practise it in *deep* water.

Stage one, resting

The pupil stands with feet astride and knees bent for balance. The head is dropped forward and the arms are placed in a 'Y' position on the water surface.

Stage two, getting ready

When the pupil needs to breathe, he presses his arms gently down, to lift the head.

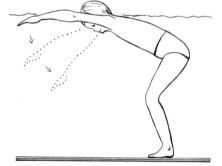

Resting

Getting ready

Exhale and inhale

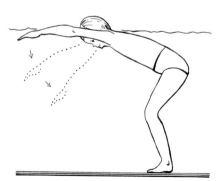

Return to resting

Stage three, the exhale and inhale

The pupil should start to exhale through the nose as his hand lifts and finish as it emerges above water. An inbreath is then taken through the mouth and the mouth should be sealed to keep air in the body for a short time.

Stage four, return to resting

The pupil returns to the stage one position until more air is needed.

Having mastered the breathing technique with their feet on the bottom of the pool, the pupils should proceed to deep water.

(N.B. It is important for pupils to keep their eyes open if possible during the four stages.)

RESISTANCE AND PROPULSION

A swimmer, in order to swim faster, must minimise resistance, increase propulsion, or both.

1   Resistance

Resistance to forward movement can be minimised by the swimmer controlling his *body shape* and position as he moves through water. Little can be done to alter body shape other than by body building or dieting. But the body position can be changed in order to streamline it as effectively as possible and thus create less resistance. The flatter the body position the better, but it has also to be adapted according to the stroke being swum, for example a front crawl swimmer should be flatter in the water than a breaststroke swimmer. The bow wave is a means of frontal resistance. The less the resistance and the better the position, the smaller the bow wave.

The teacher should help the pupil to understand the principle that the more horizontal the body is the better, provided the limb movements remain effective. Swimming costumes should fit closely too as these can create a drogue effect and long hair can also cause resistance.

2   Propulsion

Propulsion is the force that drives the swimmer forward and is created by the swimmer's arms and legs, though the legs' function is sometimes only a stabilising one. Maximum propulsion should be every swimmer's aim and if the principles are understood they can be adapted to suit the swimmer's individual body build, strength and competence.

a   *Grip.* The hands must grip the water and not snatch during the underwater pull. A snatched pull means the hand is slipping and not 'fixing' and the number of strokes over a given distance will be high.

b   *Action and reaction.* Newton's third Law, 'To every action there is an equal and opposite reaction', is very important. In other words, to every movement made in swimming another part of the body reacts. For example in the dolphin butterfly stroke as the legs kick downwards the hips rise and the arms pull down. In back crawl the hips swing laterally as the arms pull, the right arm pulls, the hips swing to the left and the legs swing to the right.

c   *Leverage.* The hand is used to grip the water and is often referred to as the fulcrum. The body or mass has to be moved by the power provided by muscular movement.

In all swimming strokes the swimmer should therefore be made aware of (i) the length of the arm *or* lever. (It is preferable that the arm should be slightly bent to shorten it so the swimmer can apply a stronger and more effective push.) (ii) the size of the hand *or* paddle. (It should be held firmly and kept flat to present the widest possible surface area.) (iii) that the stroke rate or count indicates a proficient pull, or otherwise. (iv) that strength and endurance also contribute to propulsion.

6 The swimming strokes

A good teacher must observe the pupils to decide how best to guide them. Each stroke can be looked at under specific headings and with practice any weaknesses can be recognised. The list below tabulates the main possible reasons for faults in particular aspects of any stroke.

GENERAL STROKE ANALYSIS

Section of stroke		Influencing factors	
1	Body position	i	Fear of the water.
		ii	Head too high or low in the water.
		iii	Ineffective leg kick.
		iv	Incorrect arm action. (At entry point, underwater stroke, or recovery.)
		v	Poor breathing. (Mis-timing or not breathing at all.)
		vi	The build of the swimmer. (e.g. The swimmer with fat around the hips often rides too high.)
		vii	The strength of the swimmer. (e.g. A strong swimmer often leans into the stroke causing a body roll.)
		viii	The flexibility of the swimmer. The more shoulder flexibility the better, as the body is usually flatter. (e.g. The back crawl swimmer with flexible shoulders can avoid body roll.)
		ix	The speed of the swimmer. There is usually a higher body position in a swimmer travelling at speed.
2	Leg action	i	What is the function of the leg kick? Does it stabilise the stroke, maintain body position, propel?
		ii	Depth of kick.
		iii	Width of kick.
		iv	Rhythm of kick.
		v	Ankle flexibility.

3	The arm action	i	What is the function of the arm action? The arms propel the body, often facilitate breathing.
		ii	Where does the hand *enter** the water? Are the hand and wrist held firmly? Is the elbow high or low on entry?
		iii	Are the hand, wrist and elbow held firmly at *catch* point or do they collapse? Are they positioned correctly for pressure backwards?
		iv	Is the pull–push part of the underwater stroke complete? Is the limb *track* correct for the stroke and is the elbow bent or straight?
		v	Is the arm *recovery* fast or slow? Does it have a stop in the rhythm? Is it wide or narrow? Are the arms bent or straight?
		vi	Are the arms strong or weak?
		vii	Is shoulder flexibility obvious?
4	Breathing	i	Does the swimmer understand the need to breathe with particular concentration on exhalation?
		ii	How does the swimmer breathe?
		iii	When in the stroke cycle does the exhalation begin and end and inhalation begin?
5	Timing	i	Does the swimmer understand the need to breathe with particular concentration on exhalation?
		ii	Is there a stop at any phase in the stroke cycle?

* See the section on definitions.

Stroke counting

N.B. Always keep a check on stroke deterioration — stroke counting will assist. The teacher tells the pupils to count how many strokes they take for certain lengths, e.g. the third and sixth lengths they swim. The pupils count the number of times their arms complete a stroke cycle for each full length. (A stroke cycle is measured from the commencement of a stroke's arm movement to its recommencement.) If the stroke count increases too much the swimmer may be 'slipping the water', that is, during the underwater phase of the stroke there is a loss of purchase.

Definitions:

Entry

The point where the hand(s) enter the water following an overwater arm recovery, as in front and back crawl, and dolphin butterfly.

Catch

At the commencement of the underwater pull (a few inches under water) the hands have to press the water firmly — this is called the catch point. Many swimmers allow their hands to slip the water at this point.

Limb track

The path the arms follow during the underwater pull of the strokes.

Recovery

This is the stage in the arm action following the underwater pull. In back and front crawl, and dolphin butterfly the overwater arm swing is the recovery. In breaststroke the recovery is the tucking of the elbows to the side of the body after the arm pull and the glide as the arms extend forwards.

THE FRONT CRAWL STROKE

Front crawl is a very popular stroke. It is a natural stroke, but has the disadvantage that the face is in the water making breathing more difficult to master.

Body position

The body should be as near the surface as possible but there should be a slight slope at the hips to keep the leg kick in the water. Only the heels

Front crawl stroke body position

should break the surface. The face is in water with the eyes looking forwards and somewhat downwards. The waterline should be at the top of the forehead. The head should be stable and rotation sideways for breathing should be rhythmic. A slight roll on the logitudinal axis is not uncommon especially with a strong armed swimmer who leans into the stroke. However, in the early stages of learning the trunk should be kept as stable as possible.

Leg action

The legs stabilise the body, maintain the body position and aid forward propulsion. They swing alternately from the hips in the vertical plane (close together to minimise resistance). The depth of the kick is normally 30–45 cm.

The downward kick commences at the hip. The knee, which is slightly bent at the start is straightened during the down kick. The foot is extended throughout.

During the upward kick the sole of the extended foot and back of the leg press up and backwards against the water. The knee is bent very slightly as the leg moves to the surface. The heels should just break the water surface.

Arm action

The arms propel the body and it is very important that maximum propulsion

Underwater view of front crawl leg kick

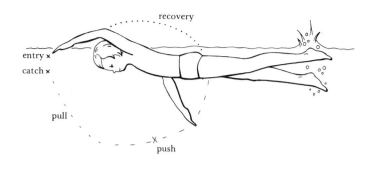

is obtained from them. The alternating movement should be continuous and one or other arm should always be engaged in the underwater pull.

Entry — the hand enters the water in advance of the head at a point between nose and shoulder line. The elbow is raised and the forearm slopes downwards to the hand which is held firmly fingers together, finger tips entering the water first. The arm is now in an ideal position to commence the backward movement with the elbow raised.

Catch — a few inches below the water surface the catch point is reached. The hand, wrist and elbow maintain their firm position as they have to act as the paddle, and slipping the water must be avoided at this stage above all.

Front crawl arm action showing entry elbow raised, fingertips first

Underwater view of front crawl arm pull

Pull — the hand, wrist and elbow are still held firmly and the hand is at right angles to the line of progression. The arm pushes back in as direct a line as possible under the body with the elbow slightly raised throughout until the thumb brushes the thigh.

Recovery — the elbow clears the water first and is lifted over the water surface to return to entry point. The recovery should be as direct as possible, i.e. the elbow bent and the arm carried over the water surface to pass near the ear. A swinging recovery can lead to a lateral swing of the hips and should be avoided.

Breathing

The swimmer should concentrate on *rolling* the head sideways, not lifting it. The inbreath should be timed to interfere with the rhythm of the stroke as little as possible. A swimmer can breathe on one side (unilateral breathing) or to the right and to the left every one and a half stroke cycles (bilateral breathing).

There are two methods of breathing which can be used in the crawl stroke whichever *side* the swimmer chooses to breathe on — *explosive* or *trickle* breathing.

Inhalation. Breathing in the bow wave

Trickle breathing

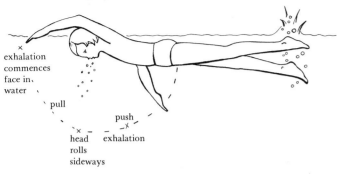

exhalation
commences
face in
water

pull

push

head
rolls
sideways

exhalation

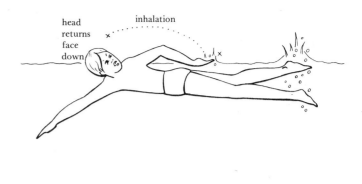

head
returns
face
down

inhalation

Explosive breathing

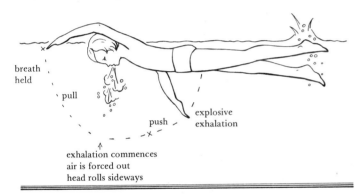

breath
held

pull

push

explosive
exhalation

exhalation commences
air is forced out
head rolls sideways

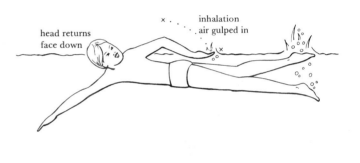

head returns
face down

inhalation
air gulped in

Trickle breathing is a more leisurely method. The breath is exhaled through the nose and mouth over a longer phase of the stroke throughout the whole underwater pull of the arm on the breathing side. Air is inhaled when the mouth has cleared the water, usually as the arm on the breathing side lifts at the commencement of recovery.

Explosive breathing is often used by a swimmer under pressure. It is a natural breathing method for competitive swimmers or tense beginners. Air is forced out towards the end of the underwater pull, i.e. when the major part of the pull is over. It is followed by a short phase of inhalation when the mouth has cleared the water.

I would recommend unilateral breathing using the *trickle* method initially for beginners as it stresses a longer phase of exhalation and inhalation. It is important for the pupil to appreciate the need to exhale at the right time.

49

Once exhalation is mastered inhalation follows automatically. Concentrate on these points:

a   Choose the favourite side for breathing.

b   When the hand on the breathing side *enters* the water, the swimmer exhales through nose and mouth. The face is held steady as the swimmer exhales, pulling the arm through the water. As the arm passes under the nose the head is rolled sideways with exhalation continuing. The hand reaches the thigh and the elbow lifts from the water. Inhalation takes place when the mouth has cleared the water. The mouth must be closed before the head returns to its original position at the end of the recovery phase.

c   This breathing phase should be repeated every cycle (e.g. measured from one arm's entry to its re-entry).

Timing

Six beats of the leg to one complete cycle. The whole arm action should flow smoothly and continuously. The six-beat leg action should give the appearance of a motor; creating a small constant splash with the heels.

SUGGESTED PROGRESSIONS FOR TEACHING THE FRONT CRAWL STROKE

Note: stress *one* teaching point rather than several at a time

Progression	Pupil organisation	Teaching points
1 Push and glide from bathside. (How far can the pupil travel on the push from the wall?)	Hands grip rail or trough feet apart on wall. Glide with arms extended and together.	Release hands from rail. Squeeze elbows to sides. Drive off with legs. Arms slide along the water surface. ('Imagine you are sliding along the top of a polished table.') Face in water, eyes open.
2 Leg kick at rail or trough. (This is a static activity. The teacher should not spend too long on it.)	Hands shoulder width apart. Elbows press into wall. Under-grasp rail or over-grasp trough. Legs should be kept together, feet stretched and near water surface.	Swing from the hips, legs close together. Stretch feet and knees. Small splash with heels. ('It should sound like a motor boat.') Check depth of kick (30–45 cm).
3 Leg kick holding one or two floats.	Check grip on float(s).	Teaching points as for 2. Check launching technique onto front.

Grip rail, feet apart on wall

Elbows tucked to side, drive off with legs

The glide position: arms slide along the water surface

Leg kick at rail

Leg kick with two floats

Launching technique; kneel and stretch keeping shoulders underwater

Grip floats firmly keeping arms extended

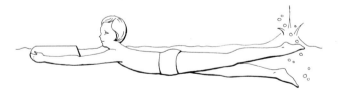

Leg kick with one float

51

Progression	Pupil organisation	Teaching points
4 Leg kick with arms extended. N.B. This is the true test of the efficiency of the leg kick and the timing of the whole stroke depends on it.	Thumbs locked and arms extended. Face in the water, head tucked between the arms. Body stretched.	Teaching points as for 2.
5 Dog paddle. This could be added earlier, e.g. at point 3 to give the idea of the whole skill.	Ask the children to show you how a dog swims.	Check stability of head. 'Balance a milk bottle on your head.' 'Blow out as you paddle.' Arm action to be kept in water. Hands firm. Arm extended in advance of head. Pull firmly. Fingers together, elbows slightly bent. Almost touch hip, squeeze elbow to side and stretch forward to commence again. Leg kick as above.
6 Arm action. Standing in the shallow end.	Lean forward, one foot in advance of other. Face in water and hold breath.	Hand firm, fingers together, fingertips entering water first, elbow raised. Check entry point — between nose and shoulder line. *Catch* point — hold hand and arm firmly. Draw a line under face and body as arm passes back. Brush thigh with thumb. Lift elbow from water. Carrying hand over surface passing near ear back to entry again. Check rhythm. Keep whole action flowing.
7 Co-ordinating the stroke. _a_ Push and glide. Thumbs locked, bring in leg action. _b_ Push and glide, thumbs locked. Bring in leg action for half a width then for the second half width bring in over water arm action; holding breath.		Check glide and leg action. Check arm action. Concentrate on steady head, and flowing rhythmic arm action.
8 Breathing standing in shallow end.	Lean forward one foot in advance of other. Put hands on knees and face in water. Space pupils so that when they roll their heads they are not looking directly at their neighbour. Practise exhaling through nose and mouth with face in water.	Concentrate on rolling the head sideways. 'Imagine your nose is on a table. Roll your head sideways to put your ear on the table.' (The pupils should discover which side they prefer to turn to.) Keep exhaling as head is rolled sideways until mouth clears water, then breathe in. ('Remember to shut your mouth before rolling your head back!') Work for a good breathing rhythm.

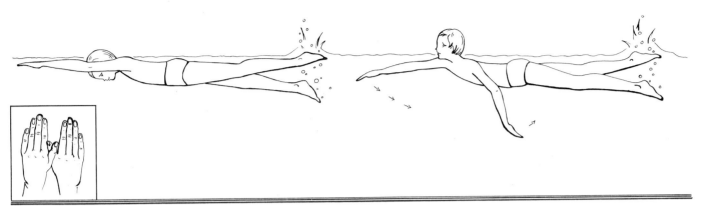

Leg kick with arms extended, thumbs locked

Dog paddle

Arm action standing in shallow water; note shoulders underwater and position of feet

Push and glide

Head steady, arms and legs co-ordinated

Introduce one breath per width maintaining continuity and rhythm of stroke; increase frequency of breathing

Progression	Pupil organisation	Teaching points
9 Front crawl arm action and breathing standing in shallow end.	Lean forward, one foot in advance of other.	Decide on breathing side. Keep face in water until arm on backward pull is passing nose. Still exhaling, roll head sideways. Begin inhaling as mouth clears water. Complete inhalation during last part of recovery. Close mouth as face re-enters water. Repeat cycle.
10 Co-ordinating the stroke. *a* Push and glide. Bring in leg kick and arm action, no breathing for a width. *b* Repeat 10*a*, but halfway across width take in one breath. *c* Build up to swimming widths breathing every cycle.	Swimming widths.	Check all teaching points. Work for continuity as breath is taken. Check continuity and rhythm. Return to earlier stages of progression if necessary.

THE BACK CRAWL STROKE

Back crawl is an attractive stroke to many beginners as breathing is simpler and the face is clear of the water.

Body position

The body should be as flat as possible but with a sufficient slope to the hips to keep the leg action under water. Only the toes should break the surface.

The head should be steady, and resting on the water with the eyes looking upwards. At speed the head often has to be raised to avoid too much water washing over the face. The shoulders are kept as steady as possible but a strong arm action often produces a longitudinal roll and makes the hips swing from side to side. An adequate leg kick will counteract much of this.

Leg action

The leg action helps to maintain the body position, acts as a stabiliser and, if the swimmer has flexible ankles, can aid propulsion.

The leg action is identical to front crawl, working on a vertical plane and using an alternating action. It is important for the legs to swing close together so that the big toes almost knock. An 'intoeing' (pigeon-toed) position is often seen when the legs have slightly inwardly rotated.

The downward kick starts at the hips with the knees and feet stretched. The knee is bent slightly on the downward kick which reaches a depth of thirty to forty-five centimetres.

In the upward kick the leg straightens. The foot is extended with the top pressing against the water until the toes reach the surface. The whole action should be rhythmic and the feet should sound like a motor. In the final part of the upward kick the leg and foot should whip to the surface fully extended.

Back crawl arm recovery

Arm action

The alternating arm action is ideal for propulsion without a 'dead spot' in the cycle. It is so continuous it is often likened to a windmill.

Entry — one arm enters the water in an extended position beyond the head and in line with the shoulder. The little finger enters the water first with the wrist flexed. (The swimmer should feel he is putting his hand on the *top* of an imaginary shelf at this point.)

Catch — a few inches below the surface the wrist and hand should maintain the firm position. Numerous swimmers let the hand collapse at this point — they should still feel as though the hand is on the shelf top.

Pull — the arm is pulled sideways following a semicircular path with the elbow bending slightly as the arm is passing the shoulder. The depth of this semicircular movement will vary between fifteen and thirty centimetres. The underwater arm action finishes when the palm of the hand reaches the thigh.

Recovery — the hand is lifted out of the water thumb first, slicing out like a blade. The extended arm is carried directly back and rotated as it passes the ear so that the little finger enters the water first.

Breathing

Breathing is easy in the back crawl as the face is clear of the water. It is usually fitted into every cycle and is fairly automatic.

Timing

Back crawl is a superbly relaxed looking stroke once the technique has been mastered. It is a flowing stroke with the arms rotating continuously. The legs beat regularly, six beats to every arm cycle. More advanced swimmers can vary this.

It is very important to the smooth rhythm that the leg kick is efficient.

SUGGESTED PROGRESSIONS FOR TEACHING THE BACK CRAWL STROKE

Progression	Pupil organisation	Teaching points
1 Push and glide from bathside and stand up.	Hands grip rail or trough, shoulder-width apart. Place feet on wall hip-width apart. Eyes up.	Explosive push-off. Body extended. Check standing up.
2 Leg kick with two floats. (Holding on the trough or rail is very difficult in a supine position, so omit static stage altogether.)	Check grip on floats, one under each arm. Launch onto backs.	Put one foot in front of other, bend knees to submerge shoulders vertically, and roll onto back. ('Imagine you're rolling over a barrel!') Kick swings from hips. Legs close together, stretched at knees and feet. Depth of the kick 30–45 cm. Splash with big toes. Constant rhythm.
3 Leg kick holding one float to chest.	As above.	As above.
4 Leg kick with head-first scull.	As above.	Leg kick points as above. (Sculling, see p. 35.)
5 Leg kick, hands on thighs.		Check body position as for glide.

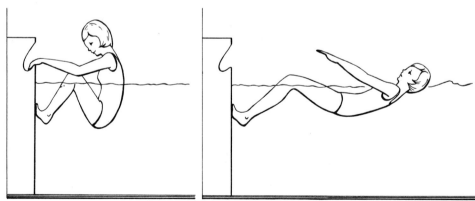

Push and glide

Glide

Stand up

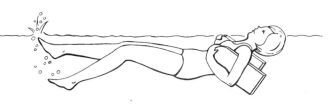

Leg kick with two floats

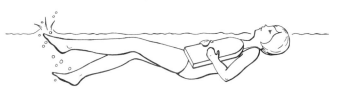

Leg kick with one float

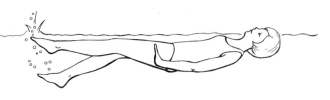

Leg kick sculling

Leg kick with hands on thighs

Progression	Pupil organisation	Teaching points
6 Leg kick, arms extended beyond head. (N.B. if a swimmer can manage this the kick will be efficient.)	Thumbs locked, head squeezed between arms.	
7 *a* Arm action at rail (N.B. The rail should be used for arm practice *only* if the swimmer is strong enough to maintain the correct body position.)	One foot under rail, the other further down the wall, underneath it. The lower foot presses into the wall, lifting the body.	Check little finger enters first. Hand firm. High wrists. Depth of semicircular sweep. Recovery direct and flowing.

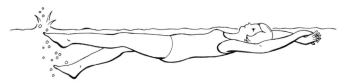

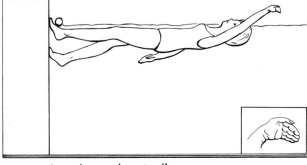

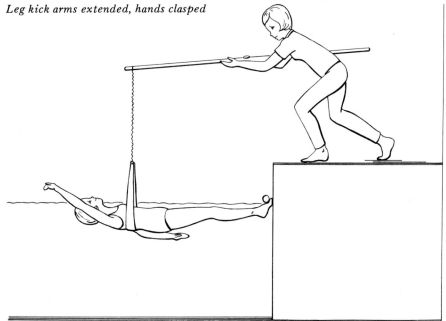

Leg kick arms extended, hands clasped

Arm action at rail
◄ Using noose and broomstick for individual work on arm action. Note position of noose
▼ Arm action standing (if there is no rail). The pupil must lean back in the water. Not too much time should be spent on this as the body position is not ideal

Progression	Pupil organisation	Teaching points
b Arm action standing.	One foot in front of other. Bend knees so shoulders are in water. One arm extended as if entering the water, the other arm by the thigh.	Check points as for 7a. Work for good alternating rhythm.
8 Co-ordinate stroke.	Push off. Glide with arms extended. Kick. Bring in arm action.	Work for smooth transfer from one progression to next. Encourage swimmer to breathe naturally. Check all teaching points.

Launching onto back 'over a barrel'

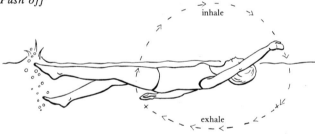

Push off

Body position and leg action

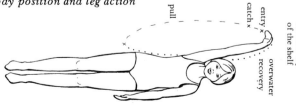

Breathing and timing

◄ *Arm action from above*

THE BREASTSTROKE

Breaststroke is a popular stroke for many beginners mainly because the head is raised naturally making breathing easy. The swimmer can also see where he is going and it is ideal as a survival stroke with most of the limb movements under water.

There have been many changes in the teaching of breaststroke, mainly in the leg action. The narrower 'whip kick' which has been developed is streamlined and very effective propulsively. The Amateur Swimming Association Law is very strict for this stroke. The body should be symmetrical with arm and leg movements simultaneous, and kept 'on the breast' with the shoulders horizontal.

Body position

The body is as stretched as possible but there is a slope to the hips to enable the leg action to take place without breaking the surface of the water. The hips are usually 15–20 cm under water. The head should be as steady as possible with the face clear of the water and the water line just fractionally above or below the mouth.

Leg action

There are two main leg kicks in breaststroke: the whip kick and the wedge kick. The whip kick is preferable from the point of view of propulsion and streamlining but it requires greater knee and ankle mobility. The wedge kick is valuable for those lacking knee joint mobility. The disabled swimmer, for example, is often more successful using the wedge kick.

The whip kick is often described in three phases, bend: turn and drive.

Bend — the legs and feet commence from an extended position (close together). The feet are drawn up towards the seat by bending and parting the knees and thighs until they are slightly wider apart than hip width. The angle between the trunk and thigh at this point is never less than 90°. The feet during this phase are sole uppermost, toes pointing backwards and they part a few inches as they travel towards the seat. They are dorsiflexed (flattened) with the toes still pointing backwards during the latter part of the bend.

Turn — this part of the kick is essential to its success as it enables the inner

The whip kick

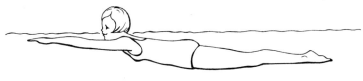 

Body position

Leg action: Bend (i)

Bend (ii)

Turn (i)

Turn (ii)

 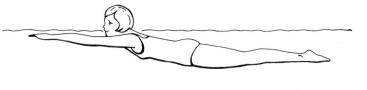

Drive

Glide

61

The wedge kick

Bend

Drive

Hands grasp trough — draw feet to seat

border of the lower legs and feet to prepare for the drive back against the water.

The feet in the dorsiflexed position are everted (cocked outwards). The soles are still facing uppermost. The inner border of the feet and lower leg present a useful surface for driving backwards.

Drive — the feet still everted and dorsiflexed commence the backward drive. The path is backwards and slightly outwards. The swimmer should concentrate on the *heels* drawing a somewhat circular pattern as they travel back-wards.

The speed of the kick is important. The feet should increase speed on the drive back so they snap together with the soles uppermost. The feet and legs should be extended and together on completion of the drive.

The wedge kick can be described in two phases, bend and drive.

Bend — the knees are bent outwards and the heels kept together with the soles of the feet facing backwards. The legs are in a diamond position at this point with around a 90° angle between the trunk and thighs.

Drive — the legs start to kick outwards with the soles of the feet pressing against the water. When the legs have extended they are squeezed together into a stretched 'glide' position.

Arm action

The arm action can also be described under three headings, pull, bend and glide.

The pull is from an extended position with the arms, hands and fingers together, and palms downwards just under the water surface. The arms are used like paddles. The hands are held firmly, elbows straight and, as the pull commences, the hands turn slightly outwards pulling sideways, backwards and somewhat downwards until reaching a point just in *front* of the shoulders with the hands slightly wider apart than shoulder width. The arms will balance the body in this position.

Bend — after the pull the arms are tucked tightly to the side of the body, elbows by the ribs, hands underneath the chin palm downwards, 'Like a dog begging'.

Breaststroke recovery — tucking the elbows into the side after the pull

start ×
catch ×

pull

1

2

The arm action:
(1) pull
(2) bend
(3) glide

3

Glide — the arms are extended forwards to a position in front of the body. There should be a slight glide before the next pull commences if the leg kick is effective, to make full use of the leg drive.

Breathing

Breathing can be trickle or explosive (see pages 65–6).

Explosive breathing is commonly used by competitive breaststroke swimmers.

Trickle breathing is preferable for the beginner and is comparatively easy to teach as the face is usually kept clear of the water.

Inhalation is taken through the mouth as the arms press downwards, sideways and backwards. This movement lifts the body slightly and is thus ideal for an in-breath. Exhalation is simple. The swimmers should feel they are 'blowing their hands forwards' into the extended arm glide position.

Breaststroke inhalation

Explosive breathing

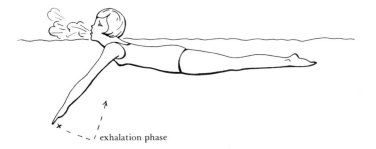

exhalation phase

breath in

Exhalation

Inhalation

Trickle breathing

start   breath in

catch

pull

blow the
hands forward

<hr>

Inhalation commences at start of pull

Exhalation commences as arms extend forward into glide

Timing:

<hr>

Pull and inhale

Bend

arm stretch
forward

leg kick
backwards

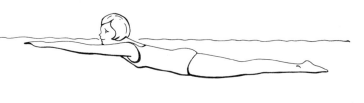

<hr>

Kick

Glide and exhale

Timing

The arms and legs are together in the glide or extended position. The arms pull and the legs remain extended. The elbows are tucked to the side and hands under the chin and, at the same time, the legs bend. The feet are turned outwards (everted) and drive backwards while the arms extend forward into the glide position. This position should be held for a short time before the cycle recommences. Inhalation takes place on the pull, exhalation on the glide.

SUGGESTED PROGRESSIONS FOR TEACHING THE BREASTSTROKE

Progression	Pupil organisation	Teaching points
1 Push and glide from the bathside.	As for front crawl (p. 50).	As for front crawl (p. 50).
2 Leg kick at rail or trough. Time must be taken to ensure the leg kick is correct.	Arms shoulder width apart, under-grasping rail, elbows pressing into wall.	Check shoulders and trunk are symmetrical.
		a Work on bend part of leg action. Knees: bend just outside hip width. Feet: soles uppermost, parted slightly and dorsiflexed.
		b Turning the feet. Now join this vital part of the stroke to the bend. Eversion should ensure insides of feet and lower leg are ready to drive back.
		c Repeat bend and turn and add *drive*. Heels play major role in narrow, backward, circular movements. Movements should increase speed until feet snap together, soles uppermost.

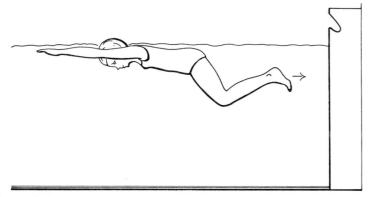

Push and glide

Leg kick at trough

Progression	Pupil organisation	Teaching points
		When feet are together and legs extended in glide, count two before commencing again. (This discourages a rushed movement.)
3 *a* Leg kick holding two floats.	Arms can be extended and hold far end of floats or elbows can be placed on float and held at 90° with hands knuckle to knuckle.	Check grip on floats. Teaching points as for 2. Check kick is symmetrical.
b Leg kick, holding one float	See above.	Teaching points as above.
c Leg kick, arms extended.	Thumbs locked. Chin resting on water surface.	Work to *reduce* number of leg kicks per width, an indication of a more efficient movement.

Leg kick with two floats

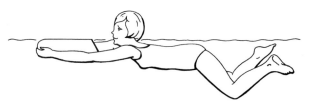

Leg kick with one float

Leg kick with arms extended, thumbs locked and head up

The co-ordinated stroke

Progression	Pupil organisation	Teaching points
4 *a* Arm action standing in shallow end.	Check stance. Lean forward, shoulders in water. Feet astride hip width, heels down, knees bent. Arms in extended position in front of body, fingers and hands together.	*a Pull* – arms straight, stopping just in front of shoulders *b Bend* elbows and tuck to side, hands palm downwards underneath chin. *c Glide* – stretch forwards under water surface.
b Arm action walking.	Shoulders should be kept beneath surface.	Teaching points as for 4*a*.
5 Arm action and breathing.	As 4*b* and add breathing (see p. 82 for breathing while standing in shallow end).	Press down – breathe *in*. As arms extend into glide 'blow the hands forward'.
6 *a* Co-ordinating the stroke.	Teacher demonstrates co-ordinated stroke. Standing on bathside in an upright position. i Arms pull. ii Elbows tuck to side, one leg bends. iii Arms extend into glide beyond head as leg kicks and snaps back.	Teacher must remind children that when standing on the bathside only one leg can be co-ordinated with the arm movement. Children must use both legs.
b Working on the co-ordinated stroke.	Children swim widths building up whole stroke. See stage 10 of crawl stroke progression (p. 54).	Work to cut down number of strokes by including a small glide in each cycle so stroke is not rushed and body remains high in water. Check continuity and rhythm. Check all teaching points.

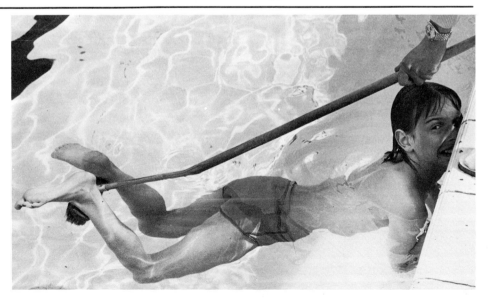

Teaching progression using broom to draw feet to seat

THE INVERTED BREASTSTROKE

It is often useful to be able to use a breaststroke leg action in the *supine* position.

If pupils have a problem learning breaststroke in the prone position they may well find it useful to start on their backs where they can watch their feet and concentrate on the relevant foot movements. It can be used to help correct an asymmetrical or screw kick. Many disabled swimmers can cope with this kick and combine it with a scull to make a stroke in which the arm and leg movements are kept in the water, good for buoyancy and stability. It is also an invaluable kick in life saving or personal survival.

The body position

There is usually a downward slope to the hips. The head is raised slightly eyes looking at the feet or at an angle of 45°. The sloping body ensures the leg movement is in the water.

Leg action

The leg action is very similar to the breaststroke kick. The legs are used to propel, balance and maintain the body position and, as in the breaststroke, the feet are important if the kick is to be effective. The feet should preferably be dorsiflexed throughout the kick.

The kick can be described in three phases, the bend, turn of the feet and kick.

Bend — the body slopes from the hips to the knees. The hips should not bend much as the movement comes mainly from the lower leg. The lower legs with the feet dorsiflexed drop from the knee so that there is an angle between the calf and thigh of almost 90°. The heels and knees should be approximately hip-width apart at this stage.

Turn — the feet evert so that the inside of the lower leg and foot is ready to press against the water during the kick exactly as in the breaststroke.

Kick — made by a drive slightly outwards, mainly backwards with the inner border of the feet and lower legs pressing hard against the water with the *heels* drawing a circular pattern. The feet should come together on completion.

The inverted breaststroke

Body position

Leg action: bend

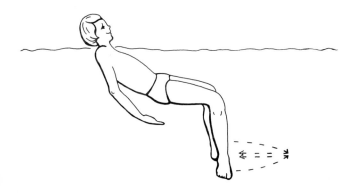

Leg action: kick

Arm action: standard scull

Arm action

The arms can (i) scull by the side of the body, (ii) remain in the water and sweep sideways from the thigh to an extended position at the side of the shoulders before sweeping back towards the thigh, or (iii) they can be lifted clear of the water simultaneously in a double back crawl arm action. I would suggest in primary schools the first two methods are the best combination with the leg kick:

Method (i). Sculling using the standard or head first method of travel (see p. 35).

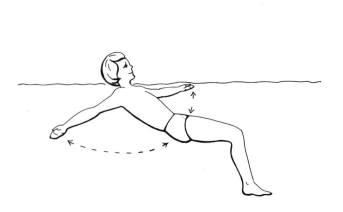

Arm action: sweep scull, arms in water

Arm action: simultaneous arm swing

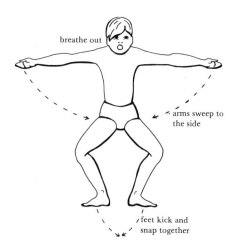

breathe out

arms sweep to
the side

feet kick and
snap together

Co-ordination of leg and arm action and breathing

Method (ii). The sweeping movement. The extended arms are by the thighs. They are both swept sideways, palm of the hand downwards, little finger leading the way to a position to the side of and level with the shoulders. The thumbs are turned upwards so that the palm of the hand is similar to a paddle. The fingers should be together, arm and hands held firmly. The arm is pressed down into the water a little before following a semicircular sweep to reach the thighs. The palms of the hands reach the thighs and the movement is repeated.

Breathing

An advantage of this stroke is that breathing is easy. It can just be kept going naturally or, if possible, fitted into the stroke. I usually tell pupils to time their breathing with the kick, 'As the knees bend breathe in and as the legs kick, blow out.'

Timing

If the sweeping arm movement is used the arms should extend from the thighs sideways as the legs bend to 90°. The kick follows and the arms sweep under water to the thighs. If a head first or standard scull is used the sculling action must be as *continuous* and rhythmic as possible and the leg action is executed as described.

THE DOLPHIN BUTTERFLY STROKE

The dolphin butterfly as we know it today is a comparatively new stroke. It was recognised as a competitive stroke in the early 1950s. It is a stroke requiring strength, flexibility and general watermanship. It is sadly often forgotten in the planning of many swimming programmes. I think it should be included for variety — adding to the depth of experience of individual swimmers. The teacher often excludes it because it might be too demanding or because of uncertainty about how to teach it. I introduce only the kick to children to start with and they invariably love the 'fish' like movements both on and under the water surface. Once they have confidence in this they can develop a long narrow breaststroke type arm action and co-ordinate it with a dolphin kick. If the entire movement is kept *in* the water, it is not so demanding. When the children become stronger they can learn the over arm recovery. For the majority of upper primary children a correctly timed two beat dolphin kick combined with an underwater arm action is adequate and far more beneficial than an overwater movement which is invariably incorrectly executed.

This is an easy stroke to teach if the teacher follows the steps suggested, although there are teachers who might introduce it by concentrating on an arm action and letting the legs react to the arm movements. Whether one emphasises legs or arms in the early stages, I hope this stroke will be considered in all timetables.

The body position

The body position is similar in many ways to that for the front crawl stroke. The water level initially should cut the top of the forehead but will vary from person to person according to physical factors. The body should be as horizontal as possible, but there should be a slope to the legs so that most of the leg kick is in the water.

The undulating body action in this stroke should be kept to a minimum. It will vary according to strength and flexibility.

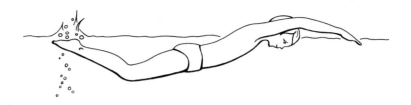

Leg action

The leg action helps to keep the body flat, aids propulsion a little and helps the swimmer cope with breathing by supporting the body. An efficient leg action also helps the continuity and effectiveness of the underwater arm pull.

The leg action is simultaneous and is initiated from the hip. The depth of kick will range from a flutter, 'tadpole' type of movement to a kick which can be deeper than the body depth. If the kick is too deep however the hips will rise and a porpoising, excessively undulating stroke will develop.

The downward kick commences with the legs slightly bent at the surface. The feet move downwards vigorously. The knees come closer together and straighten at the same time. The hips rise slightly.

The upward kick starts from the trailing leg position. Both legs with the feet together move upwards, the knees bend and will often part slightly as the feet are nearing the surface. The feet just break the water surface. An intoeing effect is often seen if the knees are parted slightly during the upward movement. (N.B. The swimmer should endeavour to keep the feet together throughout the kick.)

Arm action

The arms mainly propel the body and if they are to work effectively, strength and shoulder flexibility are advantages. The arm action can be described under the headings entry, catch, pull and recovery.

Entry — the arms are positioned in advance of the head with elbows raised slightly. The hands enter, fingers together, and wrists are firmly held and

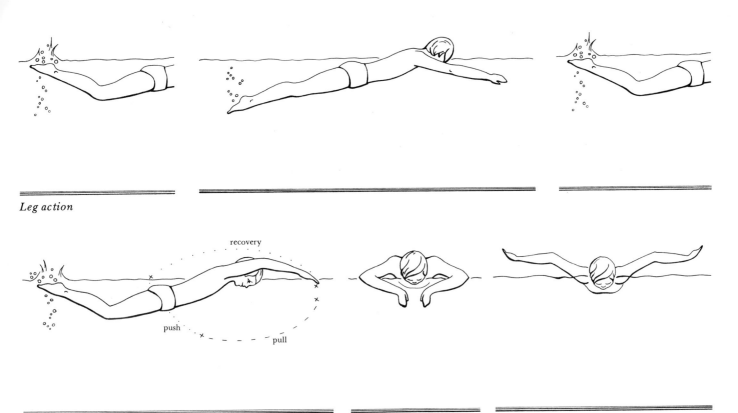

Leg action

recovery

push

pull

Arm action   *Entry*   *Recovery*

there is a slight downward slope from the elbows to the hands. The fingers enter the water first, almost together, opposite the nose or up to shoulder width apart. With weaker swimmers the slightly wider entry might enable them to cope with a V-shaped longer pull, better than with the more central entry, where the hands might slip outwards after the catch and thus miss the pull.

Catch — the arms have entered the water without a pause and move slightly downwards to the catch position. It is usually fifteen to thirty centimetres under water and the arms are usually shoulder width apart. The arms should be held firm.

Pull — the arms are still firm and push back simultaneously with the elbows raised slightly so that they press backwards. The movement is a little wider than the front crawl pull. Towards the end of the pull the hands move closer

Dolphin butterfly stroke arm recovery

together so that the thumbs almost touch. It is often called an hour glass or keyhole pull.

At the end of the pull the arms are almost extended as they reach the hips.

Recovery — the shoulders and upper arms are slightly lifted so that the elbows can lift clear of the water, little finger clearing the water first. The arms rotate as they swing over the water in the low swinging recovery. They should be almost straight. The recovery resembles a low arc clearing the water surface.

Breathing

The swimmer can breathe forwards or to the side, but if side breathing is used the swimmer must make sure the shoulders remain symmetrical. Side breathing can help to maintain a flatter body position. Forward breathing is more popular. Whichever position the swimmer chooses to breathe in it must be timed correctly with the arm cycle and leg kick. A flexible neck is an advantage.

Breathing is explosive (see p. 65) and late in this stroke. The exhalation through the nose and mouth commences during the underwater pull as the hands are passing underneath the nose and travelling towards the hips. The second beat of a two-beat dolphin stroke coincides with the start of exhala-

Breathing and timing

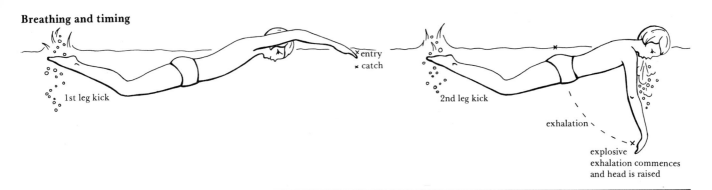

1st leg kick

entry
catch

2nd leg kick

exhalation

explosive exhalation commences and head is raised

First kick and entry

Second kick, exhalation begins as hands pass line of nose

inhalation as mouth clears water

Inhalation

Recovery-throw

tion. Inhalation takes place as the mouth clears the water at the beginning of the recovery. The head is lowered, or in side breathing rotated, back to face in the water as the arms are swinging in the low recovery.

Alternate breathing, i.e. breathing every other cycle, helps the body keep a flatter position.

Timing

Continuity of the arm action is necessary if the stroke is to be executed well. The stroke can have a one or two-beat kick to each arm cycle. It is preferable in teaching to have a two-beat kick. The swimmer should time the kicks with specific points in the arm action. The kicks should be fairly shallow.

The first down kick takes place at the start of the underwater pull, making the body flatter for it. The second beat is usually during the pull too as the arms are pressing backwards passing under the nose. The second beat gives the body position a final lift for the latter part of the pull when exhalation commences, and prevents the body being lowered or rolled unduly as the head is raised or rolled to the side for inhalation. The kicks are not always of the same strength, often the second beat is lighter. This heavy beat/light beat sequence is called major–minor kick.

The rhythm which should be continuous is 'kick, kick, throw', with breathing fitted into the cycle as above.

SUGGESTED PROGRESSIONS FOR TEACHING THE DOLPHIN BUTTERFLY STROKE

Progression	Pupil organisation	Teaching points
1 *a* Push and glide along the surface.	As for front crawl (p. 50).	As for front crawl (p. 50).
b Push and glide under water.	Stand backs to wall, sink with backs vertical and sit on heels. Rotate onto front, nose down, at same time placing feet on wall.	Blow out while submerging. Push off hard and glide. Body streamlined, head squeezed between arms, nose down, eyes open. Work for distance.
2 Leg kick at rail or trough.	Grip as for front crawl. Body sloping downwards, hips about 20–30 cm underwater. Legs and feet extended and together.	The lower legs kick together. Thighs remain steady and in line diagonally with trunk. Small splash should be seen, feet just breaking water surface.
3 Push and glide under water and add leg kick.	As for 1*b*. Arms outstretched with thumbs locked.	Start leg kick under water on front. Roll onto side and back, still kicking. Work on a small kick, mainly from the knee, in a steady rhythm.
4 Leg kick holding one or two floats.	Grip floats as described for breast-stroke (p. 68).	Head up for this activity. Chin on the water surface. Leg kick as described.
5 Leg kick with arms extended at the water surface.		Leg kick as above. Blow out frequently.
6 *a* Long, narrow breaststroke arm action, standing in shallow end.	Standing position as for breaststroke arm-action practice.	Pupils work for long, narrow pull. Arms commence from breaststroke glide position. Arms firmly held, move slightly outwards and mainly back. Raise elbows during pull by turning upper arms *inwards*. Continue pull well past shoulders. Tuck elbows to side of body speedily by rotating upper arm outwards. Extend arms forwards.
b Long, narrow breaststroke pull walking.	Shoulders under water, chin up.	

Dolphin stroke teaching progressions: *push and glide underwater*

Sink

Push

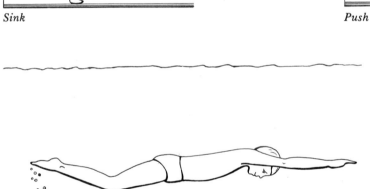

Glide

Leg kick at rail

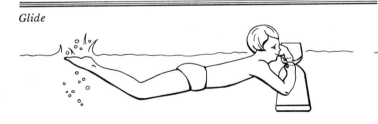

Leg kick with two floats

Leg kick with one float

Leg action with arms extended

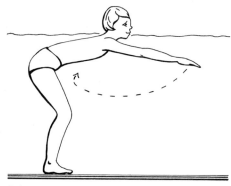

(1) Long narrow breaststroke action

Progression	*Pupil organisation*	*Teaching points*
7 Arm action only.	Swim widths.	As for 6. Chin up, body slanting slightly downwards.
8 Co-ordinate arm action and leg kick.		Chin up. Body slanting. Commence long, breaststroke arm action. Add two dolphin beat kicks. Encourage an even rhythm kick, kick–kick, kick (not **kick**, kick–**kick**, kick. First kick as arm pull commences. Second kick as arms pass under nose. Work for continuity. The full stroke rhythm should be kick, kick, stretch arms, kick, kick. . . .
9 Add breathing.	Swim widths.	Blow out as second kick starts and arms pass nose. Lift head but not shoulders (stress neck mobility). Breathe in as arms tuck to sides.

(N.B. At this point most primary children have had enough of the stroke until they are stronger. I would only add the overwater recovery for older children.)

10 *a* Overwater arm action standing in shallow end.	Standing position as for breaststroke arm action.	Hands enter water, between nose and shoulder line. Elbows raised, wrists firmly held. Draw a line backwards towards each shoulder. When arms are by hips, upper arm clears water, then lower arm with little finger leading. Swing arms forward to entry point. Repeat. Continuity is essential. Head steady, face in water.
b Overwater recovery walking in shallow end.		

(2) Elbows lift through back-wards pull

(3) Elbows tuck to sides, arms extend forwards

(4) Swimming, arm action only

Co-ordinating arm action with legs

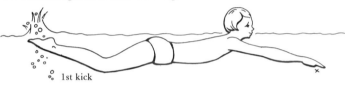 

Overwater arm action

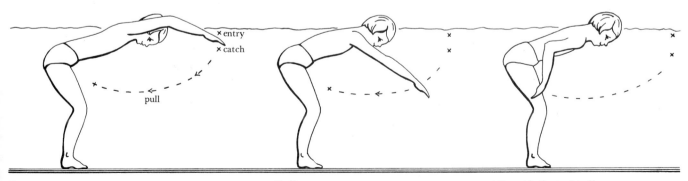

Entry *Pull* *Completion of pull*

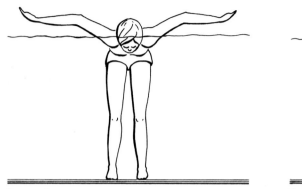

Overwater recovery

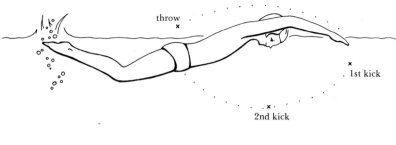

throw
×

1st kick
×

2nd kick
×

Co-ordinating arm and leg action

**Breathing
(without arm action)**

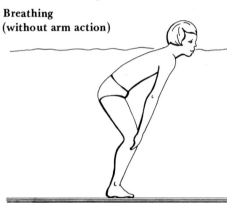

Exhale

Inhale

(with arm action)

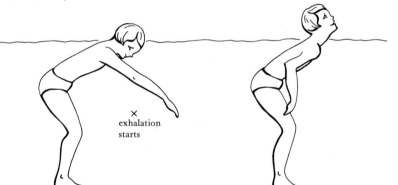

×
exhalation
starts

Exhale

Inhale

Learning breathing sequence while standing in shallow water. Keep the shoulders steady and practise rolling the head forwards and upwards and back
Entry

Progression	Pupil organisation	Teaching points
11 Co-ordinate complete stroke.	Swim widths.	No breathing yet. Glide. Bring in overwater arm action. Add two dolphin leg kicks. First kick at start of pull. Second kick as hands travel back underwater passing nose. Work for continuity and unbroken rhythm. No glide after recovery.
12 Add breathing.	Swim widths, adding *one* good breath halfway across the pool and breathholding the remainder. Work up to breathing every stroke or every other stroke.	Stress blowing *out* on the second beat and lifting head right back. Work for continuity of stroke during breathing.
13 Rhythm.		Rhythm essential.

first kick	second kick	arm throw
|	|	|
head down	blow out raise head	return head

GENERAL FAULTS AND SUGGESTED CORRECTIONS

Tabulated possible reasons for the faults with suggested corrective measures.

Fault	Cause	Correction
Body position		
1 Head too high out of water.	*a* Lack of understanding. *b* Fear.	*a* Return to early stages of stroke and build up again. *b* See 3.
2 Head too low in the water.	Effort to raise the hips. Lack of understanding. Trying to progress too quickly.	Return to body position work and early stages of stroke.
3 Fear, leading to body position faults.	Not sufficient guidance in the early stages to overcome fear.	Return to confidence activities. Build up slowly.
4 Lack of understanding of what is technically correct, leading to body position faults.	Inadequate teaching points and build up.	Revise entire stroke(s), concentrating on basic teaching points.
5 Shoulder roll.	Lack of flexibility or effort to gain more purchase from water. (Common with strong shouldered swimmers.)	With a beginner concentrate on stability of the shoulders, e.g. breathhold on front crawl with slightly wider pull. If the roll relates to a breathing fault return

Fault	Cause	Correction
	Could also relate to rolling during breathing in prone position, e.g. front crawl stroke.	to the relevant stroke and check the understanding of the technique.
6 Asymmetrical shoulders in breaststroke or dolphin butterfly.	Bad habit, or pulling more strongly on one arm than the other. Could also be due to side breathing in dolphin butterfly stroke.	Return to relevant teaching points of stroke.
7 Too buoyant hips causing them to ride too high in the water.	Body build.	Adjust head position and strength of leg kick.

Leg action

Fault	Cause	Correction
1 Overkicking and excessive splashing particularly in front and back crawl.	Poor arm propulsion leading to overuse of legs. Lack of understanding.	Revise teaching points. Flippers can often help.
2 Bending knees too much in front and back crawl.	Lack of understanding or trying too hard ('cycling').	Tighten front thigh muscles, stretch feet and knees, swing from the hip. The teacher will often have to work on these points on the bathside and guide the pupil manually first, following up immediately with practice in the water.
3 Feet not dorsiflexed sufficiently in breaststroke.	Poor ankle flexibility. Weak muscles. Lack of understanding.	The broom can be used as described on p. 69. Return to progressive leg practices and build up.
4 Too deep a kick.	Lack of understanding.	Return to progressive leg practices.
5 Too shallow a kick. 'Tadpole kick' in front and back crawl.	Weakness. Lack of knowledge.	Return to early stages of leg action. Flippers can help all strokes except breaststroke.
6 Too wide a kick.	Too large thighs. Lack of hip mobility. Lack of understanding of stroke.	Check technical knowledge. Over exaggerate narrower legs. Work on leg action generally.
7 Asymmetrical kick (breaststroke and dolphin butterfly) and/or a 'screw kick' (breaststroke).	Bad habit. Lazy leg. Anatomical problem at knee and/or hip joint. Lack of understanding.	Return to rail or trough, then with a float, build up number of kicks. With the screw kick check the knees and feet mirror each other on the bend. 'Glue' the knees and feet together at this point; kick and glide should then be *slowly* executed. Patience is required with this correction. Progress to float work for a few kicks and then stop and rest before repeating a few more kicks. Some screw kicks can be corrected by the inverted breaststroke kick in which the pupil can watch the action.

Fault	Cause	Correction
Arm action		
1 Lack of flexibility in shoulders.		Adjust the stroke to suit the individual, e.g. wider entry in back crawl.
2 Crossing over the centre line at entry in front and back crawl.	Lack of understanding.	Over exaggerate a wider entry and return to progressive practices.
3 Too wide an entry.	Lack of understanding or possible lack of strength.	Over exaggerate a narrower entry and return to progressive practices.
4 Wrist, hand, elbow incorrectly held at entry point.	Weakness or lack of knowledge.	Return to early skills and build up again. In the case of the swimmer with too short a pull, encourage him to decrease the number of strokes taken to cover a set distance.
5 Slipping the catch point.	Weakness or lack of knowledge.	Correction as for 4.
6 Too wide a pull.	Weakness or lack of knowledge.	Correction as for 4.
7 Too short a pull.	Weakness or lack of knowledge.	Correction as for 4.
8 Too long a pull in breaststroke.	Poor leg kick or lack of knowledge.	Work on leg action and progress.
9 Pulling across the centre line in the underwater pull in front crawl.	Lack of knowledge or weakness or leaning into stroke to use strength.	Revise the progressions. Over exaggerate a wider pull.
10 Too wide a recovery in front and back crawl.	Poor flexibility. Lack of knowledge.	Check teaching points. Emphasise points arm should pass during recovery, e.g. in front crawl hand and elbow pass close to head.
11 Too high a recovery in front crawl.	Lack of knowledge.	Correction as for 10.
Breathing		
1 Not breathing at all.	Tension — a non-swimmer concentrating on his stroke and neglecting breathing. Extreme effort. Lack of knowledge.	Return to early stages of confidence building. Gradually build up breathing progressions. Constant practice.
2 Wrong point of breathing in the stroke cycle.	Lack of understanding. Incorrect arm action or weak leg action.	Revise and build up efficient leg and arm actions so breathing fits in rhythmically.
3 Not breathing sufficiently.	Fear. Rushing breathing phase. Lack of knowledge.	Return to the progression for breathing in the relevant stroke cycle.

Fault	Cause	Correction
Timing		
1 Lacking in flow (appears mechanical and fragmented).	Weak leg action. Incorrect arm technique, e.g. too deep a pull in back crawl.	Return to *very* early part of the stroke and build up.
2 Co-ordination of arms and legs incorrect.	Weakness. Lack of understanding.	Corrections as for 1.

7 Survival swimming

Personal survival activities should be introduced into the swimming programme of primary children. They are purposeful, fun and aid watermanship generally. The tasks are objective and style is not vital but the more proficient the pupil is in executing the skills the less energy is used. The teacher should ensure that the children realise they are learning skills which can save their lives.

One of the greatest problems in an emergency is the loss of heat from body exposure. Energy must be carefully preserved. It must not be wasted by swimming vigorously. Clothing, except garments that are in danger of becoming waterlogged, must not be removed. It will help to preserve heat in water. Tuck trousers into socks, shirts into waist bands. Where possible button garments at the neck and at the cuffs.

Floating and drownproofing techniques are vital basic skills. (See p. 38.)

The children should also be adequately prepared to face rough water once survival skills have been learnt. Get several children to spread themselves across the shallow end and face the wall holding the rail or trough, with extended arms, then pull themselves close into the wall and push away. Repeat this again and again and the water in the pool becomes very rough.

All skills should be taught well and it is useful if the children can see them in their realistic context. Once I have taught the skills I build a story round them and the pupils go through a sequence of activities, for example a shipwreck incident.

It makes sense to work through the skills in the order in which they are likely to be required.

SURVIVAL SKILLS

a Entry.
b Moving away from the spot quickly.

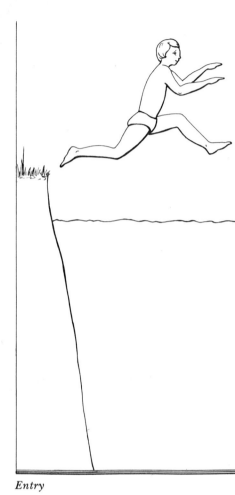

Entry

c Swimming for endurance.
d Treading water and floating.
e Surface diving.
f Underwater swimming.
g Clothing.
h Inflating of clothing.
i Exit.

a Entry (N.B. Check the water is deep enough in case some pupils cannot make shallow entries at first.)

In an unknown situation the swimmer may not know how deep the water is, or whether there are dangerous objects in it. The entry should therefore be shallow and feet first.

Several jumps are generally recommended and some are positively dangerous; it could be a painful experience to enter the water bottom first, tightly tucked up and land on a spikey rock!

In an emergency any entry can be risky but the straddle jump is probably the safest. The take off can be from a run or standing. Jump with the legs one in front of the other (not astride) and the knees bent. The eyes look forward and the top half of the body leans slightly forward with the chest well out. The arms are lifted to shoulder level and elbows bent. Some swimmers scissor kick on entry to create a resistance thus keeping them shallow.

b Moving away from the spot quickly

The swimmers shouldn't rest once in the water; the immediate area will probably be dangerous. Someone or some object might fall on them — they must move quickly. Lift the body with a strong downward breaststroke kick, pressing both arms down at the same time, and then front crawl to get away from the spot quickly. Then save energy by floating and drownproofing, and by making the best use of the clothes worn.

c Swimming for endurance

Swimmers must appreciate the need to conserve energy. In swimming strokes they should (i) breathe regularly, (ii) keep limb movements in water, (iii) swim at a non-racing pace.

Treading water

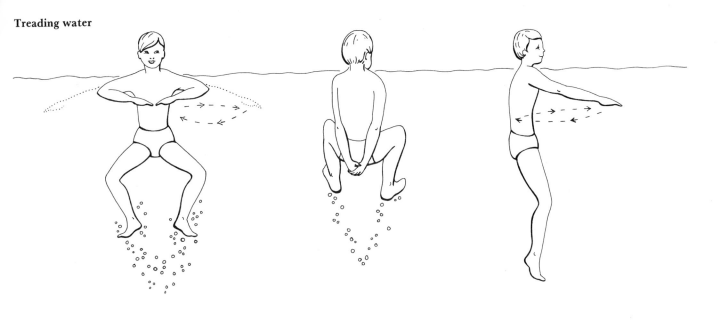

Using arms and legs　　　　　*No arms*　　　　　*No legs*

Breaststroke, back crawl, leg kick with or without sculling, dog paddle, inverted breaststroke kick with wide sweep or head-first scull are all good survival strokes. The pupil's endurance will improve as his strokes improve.

d　Treading water and floating

Treading water and floating enable the swimmer to save a certain amount of energy and to assess the situation. The swimmer remains on the spot, and in a vertical position, head just clear of the water using a breaststroke kick and sculling with the arms at the water surface. (The arm movement is not unlike smoothing sand down on the top of a table, with the arms moving simultaneously towards and away from one another like windscreen wipers.) A crawl leg kick can be used in conjunction with the arm action but mainly for variety as the kick is alternating and not directed downwards, and is more tiring.

The pupils can imagine they have injured one or two limbs and still survive by treading water with the remaining usable limbs.

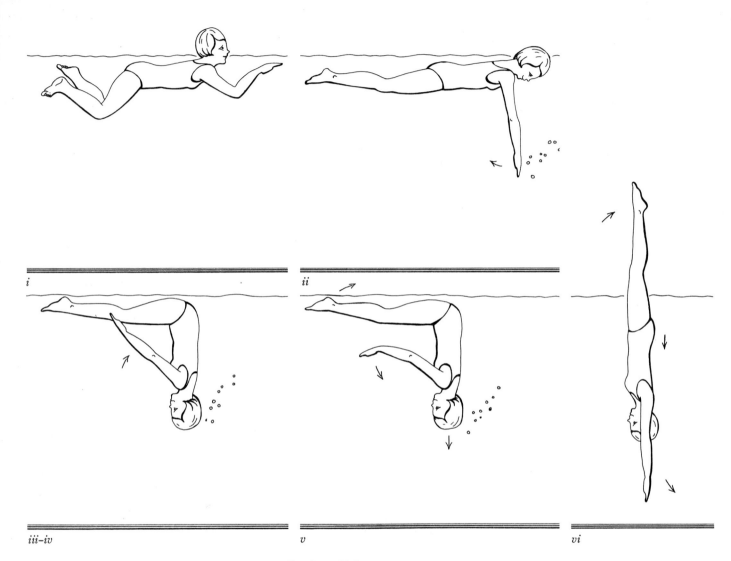

i

ii

iii–iv

v

vi

e   Surface diving

The swimmer may come face to face with danger on or under the surface so should be able to submerge head or feet first.

Head first. Sequence:
i   Swim breaststroke at speed.
ii   Look down into water.

vii Tuck

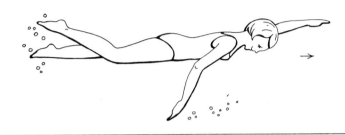

viii Swim forward, nose down

A useful exercise is to swim through a hoop before surfacing

iii   Make a strong breaststroke pull with the arms.

iv   Pike the hips into an inverted L shape. The legs and feet should be together and extended, and the arms by the hips.

v   Turn *palms downwards* and sweep arms down to an extended position in line with the head. The legs remaining straight are lifted by this movement to a vertical position.

vi   Submerge head first in a vertical and extended position.

i

ii

iii

iv

v–vi

vii Tuck, rotate and swim forward

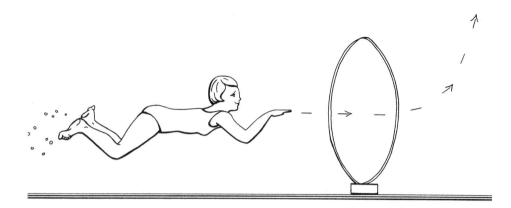

Feet first. Sequence:

i   Swim breaststroke at speed.

ii   Tuck from the prone to the head-up position.

iii   Make strong downward breaststroke kick co-ordinated with a downward press on the water, lifting the body high out of water.

iv   Stretch both arms upwards beyond the head.

v   The body now sinks in a vertical position.

vi   Remain in the extended vertical position arms above the head until deep enough to swim forwards.

A good alternative is to keep the arms by the side of the body until they have completely submerged and then turn the hands palms uppermost and sweep the extended arms upwards against the water. This also is a most effective movement in causing the body to submerge rapidly in the vertical position.

f   Underwater swimming

After head and feet-first surface dives, the swimmer should swim through and under objects such as hoops or ropes.

The secret of remaining under is to keep the *nose down* and use large breaststroke arm and leg movements. Dog paddle can be used for variety.

Inflation of clothing, trapping air in clothing

g   Clothing

Make the point that non-restricting clothing that is not waterlogged should not be removed hastily in an aquatic emergency.

Safe removal of clothing is important.

i   Upper body clothing — if possible unfasten the clothing like a jacket and remove it one arm at a time. If the clothing cannot be unfastened completely down the front it should be gathered around the neck, one arm being freed at a time, and then taken off in one movement.

Certain synthetic materials can be very dangerous and might cling to the face. Warn pupils of this danger.

ii   Lower body clothing — trousers should be unfastened at the waist and rolled down the legs to the ankles. Then by taking a deep breath *in*, the swimmer should submerge slightly to remove them.

Skirts can be kept on or removed completely.

CLOTHING REQUIRED FOR INFLATING SHOULD BE RETAINED. The shirt for example can be removed and secured around the neck before removing trousers or skirt.

94

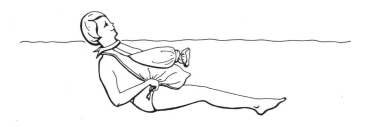

Shirt
(1) Button a long sleeved shirt at neck, back to front with
the sleeves free. Knot the ends of the sleeves
(2) Scoop air in at the tail end
(3) Trap the pocket of air by hugging the tail to the waist

Skirt
(1) A skirt can be inflated by scooping air in at the hem
(2) The air is trapped by holding the skirt close to the thighs

h   Inflating clothing

Clothing can be inflated in three main ways.
i   Trapping air into an article of clothing as it meets the water surface.

Trousers
(1) Knot each trouser leg. Gather up the waist band and blow air in to inflate

(2) It is sometimes more effective if the swimmer submerges to blow the air in.

(3) The inflated trousers can be gripped between the knees

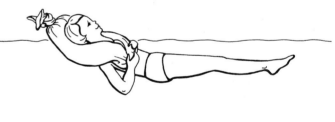

(4) They can also be positioned as shown here with a knot at the waist band. This leaves the arms and legs free

(5) Trouser legs can also be tied together, inflated and used as shown. The waist band must be kept closed

ii   Blowing air into the clothing.

iii   Plunging air into clothing by using the hand.

N.B. The teacher should tell the pupils that when there is sufficient air in the clothing they are inflating, they must grasp the opening to prevent its escape.

Diagrams illustrate methods (i), (ii) and (iii).

(1) The skirt can also be removed and in-flated. Tights can be used to seal the waist band

(2) Gather up the hem and blow air in

(3) Seal the air in at the hem and hold the skirt, blown up like a ball, close to the body

(4) Plunging air into clothing by using the hand

Inflation of clothing, blowing air in clothing

Warn the swimmers to ensure they don't go to sea with buttons missing from clothing or any holes for air to escape through. In addition to using clothing for support let the pupils experiment with various floating objects, e.g. upturned buckets, wellington boots, shopping bags, hats, floating wood, cork, car tyres.

i   Exit

The exit is as important as the entry, as assistance is not always available. Place the hands on the bathside, shoulder width apart. Submerge slightly and, using a breaststroke kick downwards, press the hands down on the bathside. The body should rise, enabling the swimmer to pull himself up on the bathside. A further kick co-ordinated with a downward press will allow the swimmer to climb out. A rope ladder should also be practised with.

Sequence

Combine the many skills mentioned into sequences of survival situations.

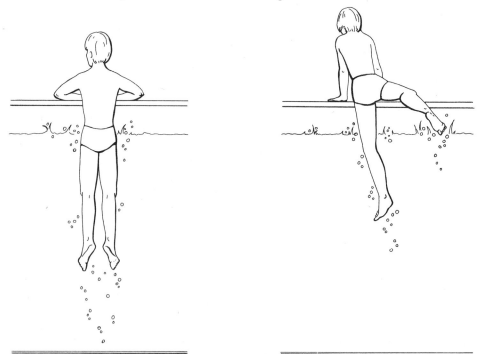

Exit

8 Diving, starting and turning

Children love to enter the water head first but before this is contemplated the teacher must check the depth is adequate. Requirements will vary according to the type of dive and, to a certain extent, the heights of pupils. A sitting dive by a young pupil where the entry is comparatively shallow can be executed in a metre depth of water but a plain header with a vertical entry might require two-and-a-half metres.

If diving is to be successful the swimmer must be confident in water and be completely at home underneath it and on the surface. If pupils are afraid of getting their faces wet they will not be happy diving. A good foundation of early confidence work is necessary.

SHALLOW END ACTIVITIES

a   *Floating*
    i   Star shape.
    ii   Tuck shape — similar to a mushroom float.
    iii Thin shape.
    iv   Move from (i) to (iii) without putting the feet down in prone and supine positions. Roll over from back to front and repeat, etc.

b   *Picking objects up*
    Picking up bricks, discs, coloured pebbles from the bottom.

c   *Body weight on the pool bottom*
    'Which part of the body can you rest on the pool bottom?' 'Move and find another part — keep moving from one part to another.'

d   *Push and glide*
    Much confidence can be gained with the streamlining positions required in push and glide.

Underwater swimming with hoops as an object to swim through

i Push and glide from the side into the prone position. Face in the water, head squeezed between the arms, body stretched. Stand up as the speed decreases.

ii Push and glide and roll over in the longitudinal axis from prone to supine.

iii Push and glide — tuck — stretch — stand up.

iv Push and glide into a front tucked somersault and stand up.

v Push and glide into a front piked somersault and stand up.

vi Push and glide under water, raise fingertips and rise to the surface.

e *Swimming through and under objects*
  i Swimming through hoops.
  ii Swimming under ropes.

f *Springing activities*
  In water of about one metre in depth.
  i Stand feet apart one in front of the other and do handstands on the pool bottom.

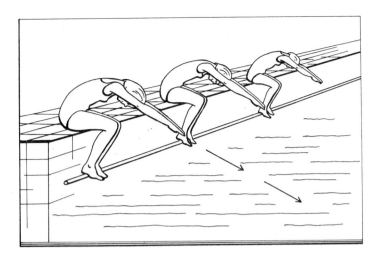

Sitting dive in cannon formation

ii   From a crouched position spring from feet to hands as in a bunny jump. Work on the spring from the pool bottom.

iii   Stand a little more erect as in a crouch dive with arms extended in a position as for a plain header. Give a gentle push from the pool bottom and land on hands. (Repeat this several times.)

g   *Jumping in*

i   Standing jumps from the bathside; the knees must 'give' slightly as the feet touch the bottom.

ii   Jumps from a short run, i.e. a couple of steps.

Simple diving skills from the bathside can now be introduced.

THE SITTING DIVE

Sit on the bathside with the heels in the trough or on the rail a few centimetres apart. Extend the arms above the head with thumbs locked and the ears squeezed between the arms. Curve the back and roll gently forwards to overbalance and the body rotates into the water. A useful teaching point is 'Touch your knees with your nose as you lean forwards and then push outwards.' The top of the head should meet the water. (Many pupils who are afraid of water lift their head, which ruins the dive.)

The water must be completely clear, and when the pupils come to the surface they should swim out of the way of other divers. They can practise sur-

Above: *The sitting dive*
Right: *The kneeling dive*

facing by turning the fingertips upwards. Then pupils can enter the water in a cannon formation, i.e. one after the other from the bathside so that the teacher can see each dive.

THE KNEELING DIVE

The pupil places one knee on the bathside and curls the toes of the other leg over the edge. The foot and knee should be side by side.

The arms are extended, ears squeezed as for the sitting dive. Lean forward, shoulders passing the knees, and keep the head down for a head-first entry.

THE LUNGE DIVE

One foot is placed on the edge of the pool, toes curled over the edge. The knee is bent. The other leg is placed further back — the distance will vary between individuals — with the ball of the foot on the ground. The arms are in the same extended position as for the sitting and kneeling dive, head squeezed between arms.

The pupil 'rocks' the weight of the body forward onto the front foot. The back leg is lifted and the body overbalances and falls forward. The front leg pushes and lifts to join the other leg so that the body enters the water diagonally with arms and both legs together.

The pupil should aim to bring the entry point a little nearer by pushing *up* more through the hips.

Lunge dive

THE CROUCH DIVE

Both feet are placed on the bathside about 15 cm apart with the toes curled over the edge. The knees are bent. In the early stages the knees will be very bent so that the body is compact and as the pupil becomes more confident the knee bend decreases. The back is curved and the head squeezed between the arms which are extended and together.

The pupils should overbalance and drive from the feet somewhat outwards. The push becomes a more upward drive as the diver improves.

THE PLUNGE DIVE

The plunge dive is required by front crawl, breaststroke and dolphin butterfly swimmers when starting from the bathside; it is also a useful lead-up to the plain header.

The pupil places the feet hip width apart, toes curled over the edge with the knees bent for stability. The back is curved with the neck following the curve of the back. The arms hang downwards by the side of the body.

The arms swing back slightly and the body weight is transferred to the balls of the feet. As the body falls forward the arms swing forward to an extended position and the legs drive back. The body is now in flight in a stretched position. The entry is several feet from the bathside and the angle approximately twenty degrees to the water surface. It is important to streamline the hands at entry. The hands should be together palms down and the neck still in line with the body and between the outstretched arms. The legs and feet are together and also stretched.

Crouch dive

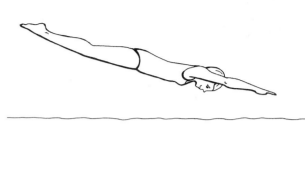

The plunge dive

Hold a streamlined glide position after entry. The glide can be maintained by keeping the body stretched with the head between the arms looking downwards. When the swimmer wishes to surface the hands can be tilted upwards and the head raised.

The pupils will find the plunge dive invaluable as a progression in learning to dive in head first and, when adapted slightly, as a racing dive.

THE PLAIN HEADER

The plain header is a more vertical dive and can be attempted when the pupils have progressed through the other dives mentioned. Check depth is sufficient.

The ready or preparatory position

The pupil should stand on the bathside in an upright position feet together, toes curled over the edge. The weight of the body should be over the feet. The arms are raised to an extended position in line with the body to make a narrow 'Y' shape. The palms of the hands face forwards and eyes look at a point just above eye level at the opposite side or end of the pool. The whole stance is firm and controlled.

The take off

The body weight is transferred to the balls of the feet. The centre of gravity

The plain header stance

The plain header (1) stance   *(2) take off*

has been consequently altered and the heels should be raised to help stability with the knees bending slightly. The toes of the feet should now be gripping the edge firmly. The knees at this stage are straightened and the feet drive upwards extending as they do so. The push up should be through the hips. The shoulders move slightly forwards and the trunk bends slightly at the hips. The hips should remain vertically above the feet. The arms still maintain the extended 'Y' position and are held in line with the trunk.

Flight

The feet have driven from the bathside or diving board at the beginning of flight and the hips are slightly bent. This hip position is maintained during flight. The rest of the body is stretched. The arms are in the 'Y' position, the legs and feet extended and together.

Just before entry the arms come together, the hands are placed side by side and the head is squeezed between the extended arms.

105

The plain header (3) flight (4) entry

Entry

The entry should be as vertical as possible. The angle of entry is governed by the angle of the diver at take off and the height of the dive.

The body remains stretched until the feet have submerged.

Teaching points for the plain header

Ready or preparatory position

a   Feet together, toes curled over the bathside.
b   Posture controlled and body erect.
c   Head in line with the body, eyes looking forwards.
d   The arms in an extended position, palms of the hands face forward.

Take off

a   Eyes still forward.
b   Body weight is transferred to the balls of the feet.

c   Knees bend and then extend.
d   Hips bend slightly.
e   Arms maintain 'Y' position and remain in line with the trunk.

Flight

a   The body at the beginning of flight is slightly bent at the hips.
b   The rest of the body is stretched, legs and feet extended and together.
c   The arms are kept in the 'Y' position until just before entry when they should be brought together and the head squeezed between the arms.

Entry

a   The body is as near vertical as possible.
b   The hips straighten as the hands enter the water.
c   The body is stretched and remains in this position until the feet have submerged.

RACING START FROM THE BATHSIDE OR STARTING BLOCK

Many pupils enjoy racing and it is for this reason that I have included racing starts and pivot turns.

With the exception of backstroke most starts are from the bathside. The depth of the breaststroke start is slightly deeper to make use of the swimming law allowing the swimmer one underwater stroke, i.e. *one* arm pull and stretch forwards and *one* leg kick before breaking the water surface with the head. Dolphin butterfly swimmers usually refrain from a deeper start despite the swimming law enabling them to kick more than once under water, because they are only allowed one arm pull before surfacing, so it isn't an advantage to remain under water kicking legs only.

Preparatory stance

A whistle is blown, usually by the referee. This is the cue for the swimmers to take up their positions at the *back* of the starting block or if the bathside is being used they stand a few feet back from the edge of the pool.

The racing start stance 'Take your marks'

The swimmer should stand about a metre back from the edge of the pool. The eyes look ahead at the pool and concentration should be fully on the race.

Ready stance

The starter says 'take your marks' and the swimmer now moves forwards to the front of the starting block or bathside. The ready position must be comfortable. The feet should be hip width apart, heels down, toes curled over the bathside or starting block. The knees are bent in a stable comfortable position to suit the individual. The swimmer leans forward curving the back with the neck following the curve of the back, but the eyes look very slightly outwards, about ten metres. The arms are in an extended position slightly in front of the shoulders with the palms of the hands facing back.

The starter waits until all swimmers are steady.

The racing start for front crawl, breast-stroke and dolphin butterfly
(1) stance
(2) take off (i)

Take off

The signal to go can be a pistol shot, whistle, the word 'GO' or a klaxon (bleep).

    The swimmer springs into action on the signal.

i   The arms swing forwards slightly and the toes automatically lift at this point. The arms move outwards and swing backwards. The body weight is transferred to the heels of the feet as the arms swing backwards and the head is lowered slightly.

ii   The arms swing downwards and forwards. The body weight is now on the balls of the feet with the toes firmly gripping the side. The body is lowered slightly before moving forwards and travelling outwards. The forward swing of the arms coincides with the outward progress of the body.

iii   The arms should be swung to an extended position just above the ears, palms downwards and thumbs quite close together. The head lifts slightly. The legs and feet are close together and extended as they drive.

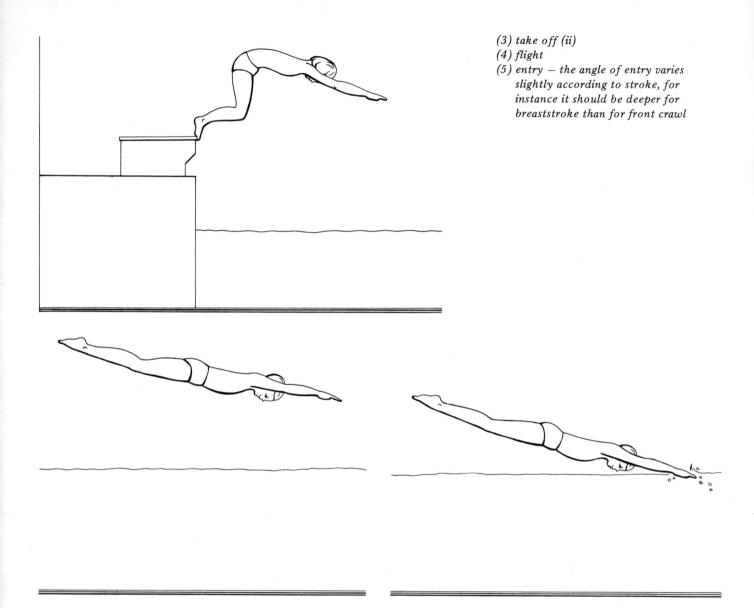

(3) take off (ii)
(4) flight
*(5) entry — the angle of entry varies
   slightly according to stroke, for
   instance it should be deeper for
   breaststroke than for front crawl*

Flight

The body should look like an arrow. It is extended and streamlined in every possible way. The body is angled slightly for entry — this will vary a little according to the stroke.

Entry

The body is still extended. The fingers enter the water first palms downwards and arms stretched. The head is squeezed between the arms. The body should be held firmly on entry.

Follow up

Each start should be followed up by a glide in a stretched position and as soon as the speed decreases the stroke commences. Advise the pupils not to overkick in front crawl before their arm action is underway. It can act as a brake to forward movement. Breathholding for the first few strokes in front crawl and dolphin butterfly is usually an advantage as the swimmer can concentrate on getting the stroke rhythm going.

THE BACK CRAWL START

The back crawl start is *in the water* but can be considered under the same headings.

The preparatory stance

The swimmers in the water place their hands shoulder width apart on the rail, in the trough, or on the bathside, or gripping the starting-block handles.
   The swimmer must face the wall and place the balls of the feet on it under the water surface. The feet should be apart, either on the same level or one foot a little higher than the other — this gives stability. The knees are in a tucked position; the body is compact but comfortable with the arms extended as the hands grip the starting point. The eyes should look straight ahead at a point on the wall.

Ready stance

As soon as the swimmer hears the command 'Take your marks' he pulls himself closer to the wall by bending his elbows, curving his back a little more and tucking his chin in. The body is lifted right out of the water at this point. When all competitors are still, the starting signal will be given.

Back crawl start
(1) Ready
(2) Take your marks

111

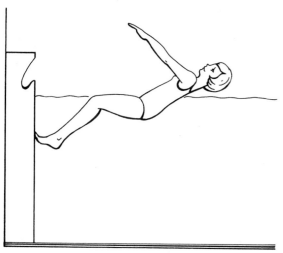

(3) 'Go' – drive off

(4) Flight – with body extended but slightly arched

(5) Glide

(6) Start leg and arm action (one arm remains extended as other starts pull)

Take off

At the signal 'Go', the swimmer drives off the wall like a rocket. He thrusts from the wall by driving the balls of his feet hard into it. The knees are straightened and feet extended. At the same time the hands are released from the wall and the arms swing sideways and backwards over the surface to an extended position beyond the head. The head is uncurled from the tucked position and stretched backwards.

The legs, arms, body and head *all* spring into action together on the signal, and co-ordination must be practised. N.B. It is important to check the hips are driven slightly upwards but mainly outwards at take off.

Flight

The body is extended but slightly arched backwards in flight, with the arms and legs together, feet stretched.

Entry

The hands should enter the water first. The body should enter the water at a slight angle so that the swimmer can glide a little under water. The body should be extended, head tucked between the arms and slightly back. It should go no deeper than forty-five centimetres.

Follow up

The swimmer will glide in a stretched position until normal swimming speed returns and then start the legs kicking. At the same time one arm should start the underwater pull, leaving the other arm extended beyond the head, and then the stroke alternates in the normal way.

TEACHING THE START

a   Front crawl, butterfly and breaststroke

1   The swimmer should be able to plunge dive before learning a racing start from the bathside.
2   The plunge can develop with the emphasis on streamlining, shallow entry, and glide.
3   Check the racing start stance.
4   Make sure the depth of dive is right for the stroke being performed.
5   Work on picking up the stroke rhythm after the glide. This requires much practice.
6   The pupils should experience the various different starting signals and variations of the length of time between 'Take your marks' and 'Go'.
7   Push and glide work generally in the water from the bathside is valuable to provide the necessary feeling of extension at take off, flight, and

entry. Breathholding for the few strokes following push and glide can also be introduced.

b   Back crawl stroke

Follow the same progressions adapted to cover starting in the water.
For all starts.
The class can work lengthways, i.e. so many swimmers step forward on the bathside and start and swim up the pool in wave formation. The second rank step forward and so on.
or
The class can work widthways. They can all go at the same time or, starting at one end, go in one after the other down the line, in the cannon formation.

TEACHING POINTS FOR STARTS

1   The front crawl, butterfly and breaststroke

The preparatory stance

Check the concentration of the swimmer. Upright stance, eyes forward on the course.

The ready stance

a   The feet positioned hip width apart and toes gripping the edge.
b   Knees bent for balance.
c   Back curved.
d   Neck following the curve of the back, but eyes look slightly outwards.
e   Arms in an extended position held in readiness for the swing.
f   Listen attentively for the signal to start, remembering the length of time between 'Take your marks' and the signal to go may vary considerably. A good starter will vary the length of time to prevent any swimmer gaining an advantage.
N.B. The take off can affect the flight considerably. Many swimmers pike in flight because they don't swing their arms far enough through on entry, or they aim their entry target at take off a little too far out from the side.

The flight

Keep the body stretched and streamlined throughout. The body should look like an arrow with feet and legs together and stretched; the arms can be extended and together or extended and slightly apart.

The entry and follow up

a   Keep stretched and check the angle is suitable for the stroke.
b   Time the commencement of the swimming stroke at the point where the speed drops to swimming speed. Avoid starting this first stroke too soon as this loses the advantage of a streamlined glide.
c   The swimmer may need to find the ideal depth to suit his size and the stroke.
d   Check breathholding while getting into the stroke rhythm.

2   The back crawl

The preparatory stance

a   Check the concentration of the swimmer, eyes on the wall.
b   Feet slightly apart for stability under the surface.
c   Do not overtense at this point.

The ready stance

a   Listen for the 'Take your marks' signal.
b   Pull up closer to the wall on the signal — body curled and head tucked in slightly.

The take off

a   The signal to 'Go' should cause a dynamic reaction from the swimmer. The drive should be hard.
b   The drive from the wall and swing back of the arms should be co-ordinated.
c   The head should uncurl and help to lead the way.

The flight

a   The head is back and tucked between the extended arms.
b   The body should be slightly arched.
c   The arms should be as close together and as stretched out as possible.
d   The feet and legs should be together and stretched.

The entry and follow up

a   The swimmer should remain stretched at entry, placing the head in an ideal position, not too far back as that would cause too deep an entry, or too tucked in as that would cause resistance.

b   The body must be at a sufficient depth to glide in an extended position under water.

c   Carefully check that as the leg kick starts *one* arm remains extended and *one* arm commences the semicircular sweep to the thighs so that the stroke thythm is immediately achieved. N.B. Many swimmers tend to pull both arms together and simultaneously to the side at this point and they delay getting into the stroke rhythm.

d   Swimmers with sinus problems may find the 'push offs' troublesome. They should *exhale* at this point and consider wearing a nose clip.

TURNING

Turns are vital to any swimmer and can make a difference between winning and losing a race.

Primary children should be shown how to negotiate the wall as soon as they have developed their strokes sufficiently.

I recommend a simple pivot for all strokes.

The following parts of the turn should be considered:

1   The approach.
2   The turn.
3   The drive off.
4   The follow up.

The pivot turn is a spinning movement with the body tucked up.

The front crawl pivot turn

The freestyle swimmer is allowed to touch the end of the pool with any part of the body. A pivot turner will use his hands at the touch.

The approach

a   The swimmer should approach the wall at full speed.

b   When the swimmer's head is approximately an arm's length away from the wall the leading arm, e.g. the right arm, stretches out ready to touch

Front crawl pivot turn

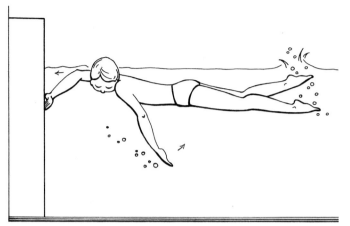

Approach (i)

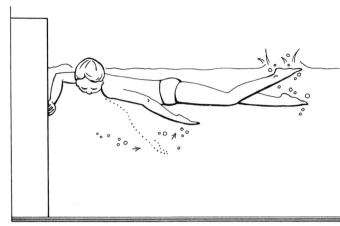

Approach (ii)

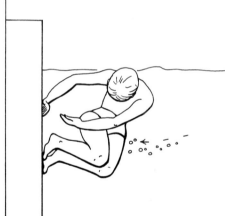

Turn

the wall. The palm of the right hand should touch with the fingertips pointing sideways, i.e. to the left. I usually say to children it is their indicator and points the way they wish to turn.

c   The left arm pushes back as in the normal front crawl underwater stroke. The body at this point moves closer to the wall and the right arm bends. The swimmer's head is now also close to the wall, face in the water, eyes looking slightly forwards.

The turn

a   The body is tucked *tightly*, knees to the chest.
b   The left arm acts as a paddle and is essential to aid the pivot. The palm of the left hand held firmly sweeps across the waist to the right side of the body. The body will be pivoting to the left. The right hand presses hard into the wall and pushes out behind the right shoulder, completing the spin.

The drive off

a   The body is a little lower in the water at this point and tucked up. The arms are squeezed to the side of the body, palms downwards, hands to the side of the ears.
b   The feet are placed on the wall hip-width apart. The balls of the feet prepare for the drive.

Drive off

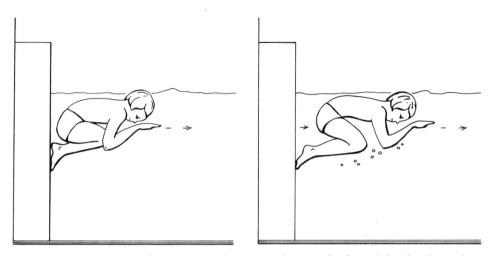

c The arms stretch forwards at the same time as the legs drive backwards. The body is now in a streamlined glide position. This position is held with the head tucked between the arms until the speed of the glide drops to swimming speed. The follow up is identical to the follow up for the start.

The breaststroke and dolphin butterfly pivot turns

In breaststroke and dolphin butterfly two hands must touch the wall simultaneously and on the same level. In the breaststroke push off a swimmer is allowed one complete stroke underwater before the head breaks the water surface. The sequence usually is (*a*) glide from the push off, (*b*) a strong arm-pull keeping the face down, (*c*) the arms and legs bend, and (*d*) as the arms stretch forward the legs kick backwards and the head is raised thus completing the one underwater stroke, after which the water surface must be broken. The push off is consequently a little deeper in the breaststroke so that the swimmer makes full use of the underwater stroke.

 The dolphin butterfly push off is shallower than the breaststroke because the law allows the swimmer to use as many leg kicks as he wishes underwater, but only one underwater arm-pull, to bring him to the surface. The swimmer does not wish to stay underwater just kicking, so generally does not dive deeply in order to get back into the stroke quickly.

The approach (for dolphin and breaststroke)

a The swimmer approaches the wall at full speed.

Breaststroke pivot turn

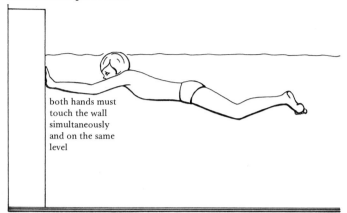

both hands must touch the wall simultaneously and on the same level

Touch

Turn

Drive off

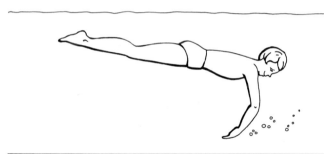

Pull

b	The touch is made with the body on the front and both hands flat on the wall.
c	As the touch is made the body tucks and the elbows are bent slightly.

The turn

a	The arms push away to one side, i.e. to the side opposite the direction of the turn.
b	The head is raised slightly and the body sinks slightly.
c	The body is still tucked during the turn.
d	The opposite hand to that used for the pivot often sculls during the turn to aid balance and keep the body near the wall.

One complete stroke

Glide and break surface

Dolphin pivot turn

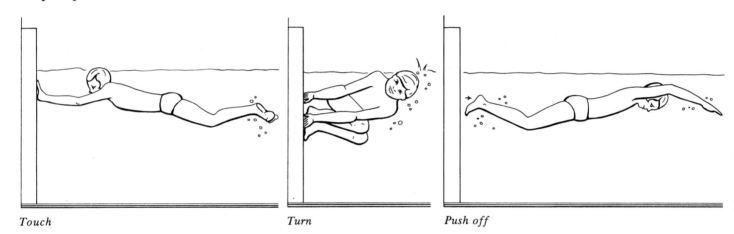

Touch   *Turn*   *Push off*

The drive off

a   The feet are planted on the wall as for the front crawl.
b   A breath is taken and the head is placed between the arms ready for the push off.
c   The push off is similar to the front crawl stroke with the depth variations mentioned. The body must be on the breast at the push.

The follow up

It is desirable to breath hold for the first few strokes and pull strongly to get into the rhythm.

Breaststroke turn

The back crawl pivot turn (basic head-up pivot)

The body should be on the back at the touch and push off in this turn.

The approach

a   The swimmer should approach the wall at full speed.

b   The leading arm, e.g. the left arm is stretched back and the palm of the hand touches the wall fingertips uppermost just under the water surface. The right arm continues the underwater arm-pull as in a normal stroke. This helps the body balance and to get closer to the wall.

c   The head is slightly *back* in the water.

The turn

a   The right arm is still aiding the balance.

b   The knees tuck (say to the pupils: 'knees to chin', never 'chin to knees' — a common mistake causing the fault of turning onto the front).

c   The swimmer should be in a tucked position slightly on his back.

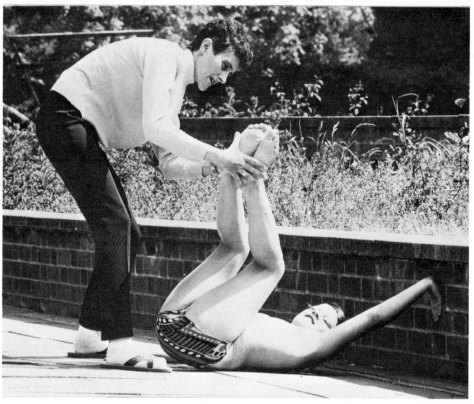

Back crawl turn, approach — touch

d   The tucked legs swing near the water surface to the side of the leading arm — i.e. the left side in this example. (I often tell the swimmers to imagine they are sitting on a plate and they are to spin to one side or the other.)

e   The hands are gathered near the head, palms up.

The drive off

a   The body is still tucked. The feet planted on the wall slightly apart ready for the drive.

b   The arms are extended backwards, palms of the hands uppermost as if the arms, head, seat and feet are pushing and gliding along a polished table top. Many pupils swing the arms out of the water at this stage but they should keep their arms in the water.

c   The legs and body stretch at the same time as the arms extend.

Back crawl pivot turn

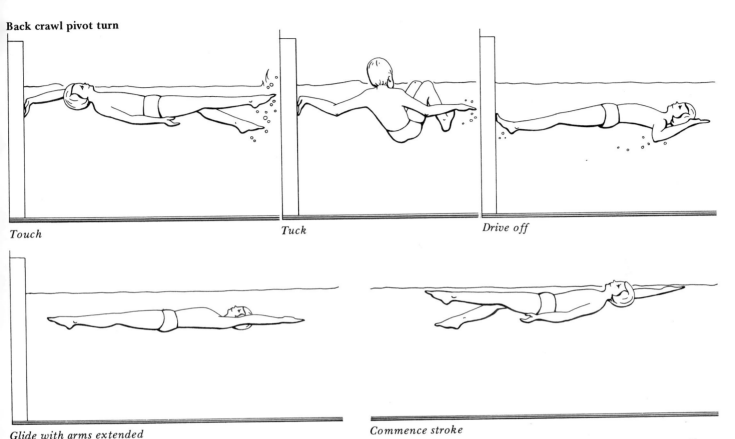

Touch   *Tuck*   *Drive off*

Glide with arms extended   *Commence stroke*

d   The body is now in a streamlined position gliding away from the wall.

The follow up

The follow up after the glide is identical to the follow up after the start.

Marker flags are used in competitions for backstroke swimmers to warn them when they are near the wall for their turn. Teachers can guide pupils in this respect by getting them to swim set distances and count their strokes. Eventually they will know by the stroke count when they must prepare for the turn.

Teaching the turns

The class should be spaced out several yards from the wall. There are several suggestions for pool layout for turn practice — the class can work widthways or lengthways:

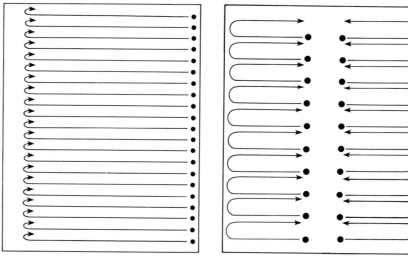

Individual work

Pairs working back to back. An element of competition can be introduced

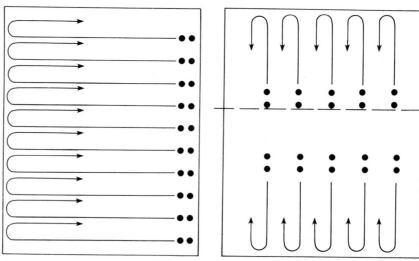

Pairs working alternately. Widths with turns can be timed.

Two groups working on turns in alternate   of five at each end

9 The school swimming competition

The ideas in this chapter are a basic guide to a teacher wishing to organise a *simple* competition in school.

It is important for those organising and competing to recognise and abide by Amateur Swimming Association laws. This ensures a uniformity in the events. A detailed guide on organising a swimming gala and the A.S.A. laws is obtainable from the Amateur Swimming Association.

Before the competition:

1 Elect a small working party to help in the organisation with a gala secretary and treasurer.
2 Consider: The length and content of programme. Are events all racing? Is there to be diving, a novelty race, etc.?
Age and ability of the pupils.
Officials — where are they coming from — school/club?
3 Equipment:
Starting pistols and cartridges.
Whistles.
Stop watches.
Clip boards.
Judges.
Timekeepers. } slips
Chief officials.
Recorder sheets and sheets of spare paper, sticky tape.
Programmes.
Coloured chalks, duster, blackboard, scoreboard.
Pencils, ballpoint pens, etc.
Novelty race equipment.
Lane ropes.

Lane numbers (waste paper baskets upside down numbered clearly on the side are suitable).

False-start ropes (this is a rope placed widthways near the start of a race, at a distance fixed by the A.S.A. law; if there is a false start it is dropped to recall the swimmers).

Backstroke ropes.

Starting blocks.

Possibly — rubber rings, arm bands.

Gramophone or tape recorder.

Records or tapes.

Tables for officials, e.g. recorder, announcer, etc.

Chairs for officials.

Certificates, medals, cups (prepare long before competition day).

Competition

Officials to be appointed.

a   A referee.
b   A starter.
c   A check starter if there are handicap races.
d   A chief judge.
e   Not less than two placing judges.
f   Not less than two turning judges.

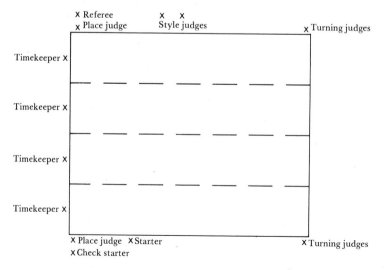

SCHOOL MATCH RECORDING SHEET

COMPETITION _____ v. _____

DATE _____ TIME _____

Event number	Event	School				School		
		Position	Time	Points		Position	Time	Points
1		A				A		
		B				B		
2		A				A		
		B				B		
3		A				A		
		B				B		
4		A				A		
		B				B		
5		A				A		
		B				B		
6		A				A		
		B				B		
7		A				A		
		B				B		
8		A				A		
		B				B		
9		A				A		
		B				B		
10		A				A		
		B				B		
		Points Total				Points Total		

Final Result: School Placing	Total Points
1st _____	_____
2nd _____	_____

Points scoring:	1st	2nd	3rd	4th
Individual events	6	4	2	1
Team events	10	7	5	3

g   A chief timekeeper and sufficient timekeepers to ensure the necessary swimmers are chosen for the final.

h   Competitors' stewards.

i   Recorders.

j   Style judges (if required).

NB. In competitive swimming lane one is on the *right* as the competitors face the start of the course

---

JUDGES

EVENT NUMBER

LANE	POSITION
1	————————
2	————————
3	————————
4	————————

COMPLETE SLIP TO THE RECORDER

EVENT NUMBER

LANE	POSITION	TIME
1	————————	————————
2	————————	————————
3	————————	————————
4	————————	————————

TIMEKEEPER

EVENT NUMBER

LANE NUMBER

TIME

Appendix

Awards

Awards indicating the standard and level of swimming achievement are available for the able and disabled in all aspects of swimming — general proficiency, speed, survival, synchronised swimming, diving, water polo, etc. There are special conditions for the handicapped in some awards in addition to specific awards for the handicapped.

Awards are at intervals changed completely, revised, or have additional grades and skills added. It is for this reason that I have not detailed conditions here. I would advise teachers to contact the national body concerned when they require the latest information. Gay wall charts and detailed lists of conditions are available for the school notice board. Some schools and Education Authorities provide their own certificates to motivate the pupils in the early stages.

Teachers should not design their school swimming programme around awards. A general, sound programme will be far more suitable and if the leading-up stages are well taught, the necessary skills for each aspect of swimming should be more than adequately covered.

Suggested music for water activities

Sculling to music: Head first.
Feet first.
On the spot.
Side Saddle, Russ Conway.
Submerging to music: *Song of the Narobi Trio*, Hot Butter.
Rotation and sculling to music: *We're the Maoris* (*Hoea Ra*), Rolf Harris.
Breaststroke into a front tuck, somersault to music: *Morning Town Ride*, the Seekers.
Sequence (e.g. tub-sculling, log roll) to music: *Love is Blue*, Paul Mauriat.

Some useful addresses

The Amateur Swimming Association, Harold Fern House, Derby Square, Loughborough, LE11 0AL. (Tel.: Loughborough 30431).

The Physical Education Association of Great Britain and Northern Ireland, Ling House, 10 Nottingham Place, London W1M 4AX. (Tel.: 01–486–1301–2).

Bibliography

1   *The Teaching of Swimming*, Amateur Swimming Association.

2   *Better Swimming for Boys and Girls,* Helen Elkington and Tony Holmyard, London Kaye and Ward Limited.

3   'Swimming is Fun', Helen Elkington, *Swimming Times,* March 1970.
    'Multi Stroke Teaching Method', Helen Elkington, *Swimming Times*, June 1970.

4   'The Effective Use of the Pool', Helen Elkington, *Journal of the Chartered Society of Physiotherapy,* October 1971.

5   'Synchronised Swimming in the School Swimming Programme', Helen Elkington, *Journal of the Physical Education Association,* May–June 1974.